AF230289

Contents

Illustrations

1. Cover: What they each see!
2. The mesmerized waist high young lad follows along on the knife scraper eating utensil as his grandpa tells him the epic folklore tale.
3. The upset waist high young maiden is 'madly marching' towards the other miserable weary trekkers who have to go around her held up lead family.
4. The hungry saber-toothed cat decided to have his own picnic snack, cornering the plumpest fleeing Mammoth People picnicker.
5. The Mammoth People lead family is cooperating to rescue the struggling fair young maiden and is reflecting off of the left side of the kneeling nervous lead mammoth's head.
6. The waist high young maiden's frightened kitty has just scratched grandpa's face making him more delirious than he already was because he thought that he was seeing the roaring male lion volcanic ash cloud that close up.
7. The lead family as they trekked in the long Mammoth People mammoth caravan to...'here'.
8. Mom and dad had no warning or chance to stop the domestic milk cow from bucking away from them with the pair of lions on her back.
9. The pesky house rat took advantage of the time that grandma spent away from the cottage when she had to get fresh warm cow's milk for her crying infant grandchild.
10. Concentrating grandma is steering the submerged swimming lead mammoth after they rescued the entire lead family....after the 'epic deluge' swept them away.
11. There's so much going on during the 'powwow' that even the nervous lead mammoth needs reassurance as she continually sniffs over the lead hunter herders shoulders towards his bearded face.
12. It's usually a pack or a pair of dire wolves that attack the summertime picnic event.

Acknowledgements

First and foremost, I'd like to acknowledge the sacrifices that my dear wife Janet made in my absences the last eight years. I say absence because I was truly living in two worlds throughout my research which robbed her of much of our time together and for that I'm deeply sorry but truly appreciative. She was the lifeline between me and the rest of our family and our community while I was submersed in discovery. There's no question that the annoying background noise of her rustling around me while I wrote up interpretations at our kitchen island table deep in thought, helped me stay grounded in this epoch.

I'd like to thank my daughter Michaela (Hruska) Wachal for giving her precious time to do a proof read of my first draft and first attempt at a book... and yes, I definitely needed to make shorter sentences and more paragraphs.

I'd also like to give special thanks to my banker friends Steve Cleveland and Emily Rischling for all of their help in formatting the book for self-publication and for the e-book. I know that I couldn't have done it without them. That's because I am for all intents and purposes just a 'farmer' who has always had a passion for figuring out what really took place in our past, and my computer skills are minimal to say the least.

The microlithic abstract art figurative language was figured out from a lifetime of private but ultimately intense research and was discovered from the soil up with only self-learned archaeological context. I'm not trying to be offensive by saying so, but that reason alone may be the very one that enabled me to decipher it......"it just is what it is".

The Sentient Mammoth People

Mark Hruska

"This book was written in an effort to verify and present a clearer understanding of one of our planets ancient past civilized cultures. The realization that we are inferior to them is the only way to change our arrogance..."

Preface

"A singular strength of mind is required to enable a man to live among others consistently with his own ideas and convictions, to be master of himself, and not to fall into the habits or exhibit the same passions as those with whom he associates."
-Baruch Spinoza (1632-77)

If not for accidentally having stumbled on this seventeenth century Portuguese Jew rationalist's quote in a farm magazine while waiting at the bank to visit with my loan officer during the spring of 2010, I doubt I would have ever achieved the state of rational cognition that was required to continue working on the discovery that I had intentionally embraced upon and was diligently figuring out earlier that winter. It was December of 2009 when we had a blizzard that left me housebound and alone for three days. This was just the spark that I needed to get started on the project that I had been waiting a lifetime to delve into.

Since about the age of ten or earlier I was always interested in looking for 'arrowheads', as we called them back then, not knowing that many if not most of them were actually spear or atlatl points. I'd walk or ride my bike down to the river that was only about a half mile from our small one bathroom ranch style house and throw my bamboo fishing poles line and sinker into the muddy river. Then I would climb back up its muddy bank and go look for 'arrowheads' on the adjacent tilled farmland. What really sparked my interest though was when my cigar chewing grandfather brought unwashed arrowheads in a cigar box to our house that was up on a hill. He always wore a summertime cap like the ones worn by locomotive engineers, and would show these arrowheads to my many siblings and me. I was the second oldest. His farm was about one mile south of ours and had the same river that also went past our place. The river wound through it creating big looping horseshoes. My grandfather at one time had to cut a ditch to drain where a low spot was and after a rain he found all of this 'stuff'! All of that 'stuff' was the single incident in my subjective child's imaginative mind that planted the seeds of wanting to 'know'. That passion for wanting to know the answers to all of my questions about the first people who had lived here took hold at that early age and never subsided, perhaps because I had an inquisitive mind. For some reason two of my brothers, one a year older and one a year younger than me, cared little for the past, while the other siblings were too young to understand. After all, the history books simply told us that the people that made that 'stuff' were just the red skinned Indians that we saw on our black and white TV's westerns.

As I matured I never lost that deep rooted desire to continue to look for artifacts. I continued to broaden my horizons out further away from the neighborhood where I grew up, where I continued to farm and eventually raise my own family. All of that 'stuff' that I collected throughout the years was always labeled with its proper site number, the first site being on my grandfather's farm where I found enough 'stuff' to have considered it a 'site'. I eventually discovered about twenty five sites that had compilations of artifacts and debitage that were in close proximity. I realized at some point when I was about forty years old, that these sites couldn't be individual Indian villages because they just weren't big enough. They were no bigger than the average homestead farm yard, but were all about a half mile to three quarters of a mile apart along the river as if they were intentionally spaced within shouting distance. Besides that, many of the sites were located exactly on the same higher elevated locations next to the river that the first historical homesteaders built their farm yards on. What's so amazing to me is that those homestead yards are now gone too and being farmed over by huge modern day farm equipment. Amongst the debris of the houses and barns that included late nineteenth century and early twentieth century pottery shards and glassware are the scattered debris of the earlier settlers who had also lived there at one time. That debris included their debitage or what I thought was the flint flakes from their flint knapping, their flint arrow and spear points, flint flake knives and thumb scrapers, bone and heat treated stone tools and their own style of potsherds.

When I got older I made a personal commitment to myself that when I reached the age of fifty I was going to figure out who those earlier people were and why they created all of the rubbing and etching on those tiny pieces of flint. I knew that at any age later then that would certainly mean a decrease in energy and in cognitive abilities. When I turned fifty and our youngest child went off to college, I started sorting and cataloguing everything that I had collected up to that point in my life. I bought stackable plastic shoeboxes from Walmart and I placed all of the sorted artifacts in Ziploc snack pack plastic bags that fit nicely in the plastic shoeboxes like cards in an index card file. I also purchased an eight diopter magnifier that you could view through with both eyes while you held the piece that you were magnifying with your left hand and still be able to write with your right hand. I knew that I had to view the rubbing and etching that was on all of the artifacts much closer up because I was acutely aware for the longest time that the folks that created this 'stuff' were purposefully making it appear the way it did for a reason....especially since so much of it didn't seem to have any utilitarian use. Some of the flint pieces were irregularly shaped with all of this rubbing and etching and many of them didn't have even one knapped or honed sharp knife edge while others had at least one honed razor sharp knife edge that would be opposite a snapped off, or 'backed' edge. They could use this 'backed' edge to press their fingers against to apply pressure to the knife edge. If they weren't using some of those seemingly useless pieces of heat treated flint as a knife scraper eating utensil or as a perforator or shaft scraper...what were they doing with them?

My inquisition went on until that life changing winter of the 2009 December blizzard, which happened to be when I was fifty three. I had waited for an excuse to go into my little basement freezer room that's no bigger than a good sized closet and is where I had moved all of the stackable plastic shoe boxes along one of its walls. Then I settled in and allowed the burning desire that I was most passionate about to take over. Who were the folks that created this 'stuff' and what exactly did they create? Because of that blizzard I sat down at my desk and peered through that magnifier...back through time. By the third day of being totally alone with only the thoughts inspired by the tiny heat treated flint stones, I was being transported back in time much further than I expected and was beginning to 'see' what those incredibly talented people were doing on a microlithic level. At that time I didn't have any idea that the word 'microlithic' even existed, nor did I have any idea what I was actually looking for other than some sign of 'art'. However, I knew what monolithic meant so I assumed that 'tiny' 'stone' would mean microlithic.

By March of 2010 the only way I kept my sanity was to take a break from my constant 'eureka' moments of discovery, and research the seventeenth century Portuguese Jew Baruch Spinoza whose rational thinking is what reinforced my own rationality. Of course that train of thought which was of a 'singular' strength of mind was going to mean a very lonely existence, but I accepted the challenge whole heartedly because of my insatiable desire or passion to know the truth. It's the only way that I was able to crawl out of the narrow-minded box that I was born into and erase everything that I had been taught from birth onward. I had to approach what I was figuring out from the perspective of someone with a cleaned slate or an open mind. That meant figuring out the origins of the art from only the art along with what was interred in the soil with it. Yes, by examining nothing more than the debris and debitage artifacts that these people left behind would be the only possible way to figure anything out. That's because these artifacts along with the levels of stratum that they had originally been laid down in had been incorporated to the depth of the plow in the tilled farm fields. The scientific method would automatically be rejected since all the levels of stratum down to the clay loess had been mixed and interred by not only the plow, but the subsequent larger and larger modern day farm machinery over the last one hundred and fifty years making it impossible to date anything by strata. Try to imagine the big sharp disk blades of today's modern farm machinery slicing into the ground at depths of up to six inches or more and moving at incredible speeds. Imagine the horrific damage they would do to any stone, bone or potsherd that they hit square on, not to mention the irreparable damage that the big tractor tires' lugs would do from the sheer weight of the tractor. Some of these fields are being disked twice a year ahead of planting, so you can clearly see how the bigger 'stuff' that I found fifty years ago has been spared by that many years of bombardment from razor sharp blades chipping and slicing through it or from simply being crushed.

There is of course another way to date some of that debris and debitage. Some of it is bone that you could get an approximate carbon date from, and even get DNA samples to determine what animals it came from. Some of the potsherds and many of the heat treated flint pieces have grey residue adhered to them that could also be analyzed for DNA and possible dating, but I wanted to examine another possibility, one that modern day archaeologists just haven't seemed to grasp. Down through the decades professors of archaeology have trained their students to think of only the meticulous scientific method as a means of verification. It was the only way to get 'empirical' evidence. They wouldn't think of instructing their students to take a toothbrush and vigorously brushing away all of that baked on grey residue along with the very sheen or the patina of the piece. To brush it clean down to the pristine surface of the beautiful heat treated fossiliferous flint stone so that they could 'see' it the way that the individual that created it actually perceived it when he was creating it all of those millennia ago...and before it was used as a utilitarian tool. In other words.....nobody seemed to be taking a 'much' closer look at the debitage and other debris and not just focusing all of their attention on the spear and arrow points and the shapes of their barbs and bases because that determined the culture that the people that made it belonged to. They have to be assuming that all of those individuals in that one culture, over their entire adult lives would never have experimented or altered the shapes of their atlatl points or spear points....or their prismatic knifes for that matter.....especially when they were so adept at working with stone.

I realized early on that it was going to be incredibly difficult to indoctrinate the world about the Mammoth People hunter herder microlithic abstract art figurative language that I had discovered because we rely on the empirical scientific method to verify discoveries. The research from a discovery has to be repeatable by other scientist and since this discovery is based on 'art' and not math, I had to figure out a method of interpretation that would allow anyone to find similar pieces that have the same repetitive themes or in this case, folklore tales on them. Only by showing repeated examples that have the same folklore tales incorporated into them will anyone take it seriously, but first they will have to be able to 'see' the art so that they too can be drawn into the storyline of the artwork....as I have.

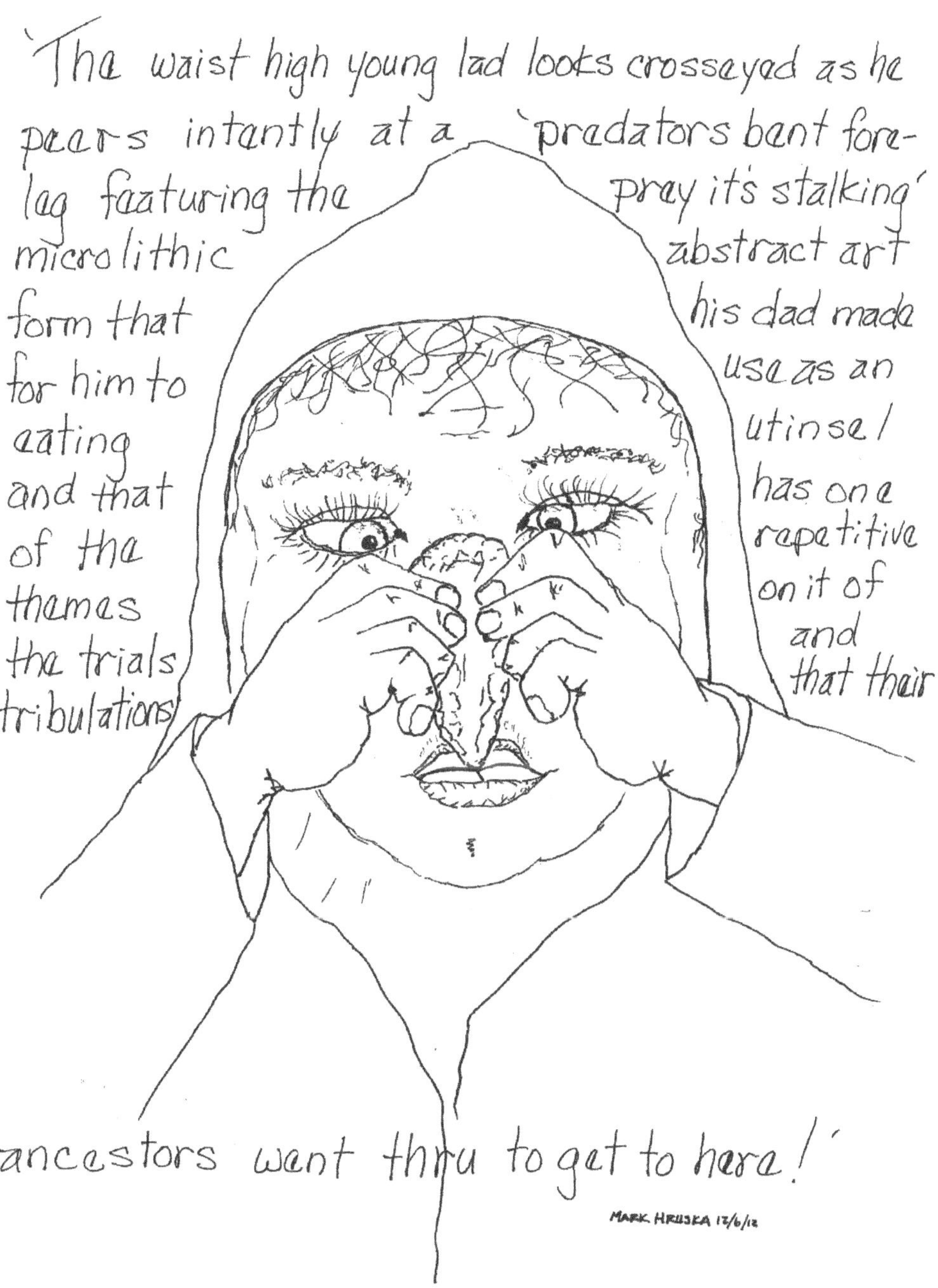

2. The mesmerized waist high young lad follows along on the knife scraper
eating utensil as his grandpa tells him the epic folklore tale.

Chapter One

Paleo Amerind Microlithic Abstract Art

This book is a description of the microlithic abstract art that I discovered starting in January of 2010 through September of 2017. It took me three months to completely figure out the Paleo Amerind Stone Age abstract art figurative language, once I was onto it. I didn't start writing up interpretations of individual pieces until about March of 2010 but I identified many artworks for what they represented. It wasn't until March of 2010 that I got serious about interpreting the hunter herder microlithic abstract art that was on individual pieces of debris and debitage that included flint end scrapers, flint knives, flint flake knives, fractured flint spear points, potsherds, and heat treated stone pieces as well as bone limestone and siltstone. I interpreted them and then wrote up the interpretations, figuring that if I just keep interpreting pieces, eventually I'd see imagery of the people who created the microlithic abstract art. I struggled to keep an open mind about what those people looked like knowingly having been stigmatized by the historical red or reddish skinned Indians from historical records. I'm not in any way being offensive by saying red skinned because I don't know any other way to describe the color of their skin in relationship to Caucasian peoples flesh colored or white skin tone. Keep in mind that for any researcher, it's extremely difficult to find what you don't know you're looking for. All I knew for certain was that the folks that made these heat treated flint tools were also making them look a certain way by doing 'unnecessary' rubbing and etching on them.

Let me describe how I first figured out that there was any art at all. I started looking closely at the entire tiny heat treated flint flake knives that appeared to be nothing more than debitage and that I absolutely knew were rubbed and etched into the shapes of birds, especially their heads. Many of these flint flake knives are less than an inch in diameter. Once I absolutely knew that Paleo man was making animal and bird shapes I got really serious about what they were exactly doing on such a small scale. I knew they were being created by Paleo people because of the prismatic knives associated with all of the other artifacts. I viewed everything through an eight diopter three inch lighted magnifier that gives at least three times magnification. I learned that the color, texture and the unique designs in the fossiliferous flint played a significant role in what kind of bird or animal that the abstract artist would try to bring out of the stone. If he saw a birds head in a translucent piece of flint he would try to create the microlithic artwork around that image.

It didn't take me long to figure out what the Stone Age artist was doing. I learned early on that scrubbing the piece clean with a toothbrush and water was essential if you wanted to read the abstract art that was on it, which goes against all archeological common sense because you'd be removing any residue and you'd be removing the patina that could also possibly help date the piece. I realized that I had to 'see' the stone the way that the artist 'saw' it in its pristine condition while he was rubbing, etching and knapping it. To clean off thirteen thousand year old caked on grey organic matter would seem sacrilegious to an archeologist but since I'm not an archeologist I did what made sense, and that's to clean it off. There is no way that you would see any of the microlithic abstract art if you didn't scrub it down to what the artist was looking at when he produced the piece. He was looking at and 'into' the stone at an incredibly tiny or 'micro' level. I'm talking 'head of a pin' level and even smaller.

Once I realized that they were seeing imagery at this 'micro' level on and in the stone and were actually producing art around it, euphoria set in and I went to work trying to figure out how they saw such small imagery. I just couldn't accept the fact that they were actually seeing it with their naked eyes at this micro level that I could only see with the aid of my eight diopter magnifier which magnifies three times my normal vision. Keep in mind that I was over fifty years old and needed reading glasses anyway and that just maybe a five year old could actually see that imagery without the aid of magnification. I was trying to figure out how those folks could magnify the stone to see minute images when I could barely make them out with my magnifier. It took at least two months of constant discovery and skeptical denial before I came to the rock solid conclusion that they simply could see at this level. Their eye sight was at least three times sharper than mine. Which started another whole line of thought about our supposedly 'cave men' ancestors. Not only did I come to realize that they had unbelievably acute eye sight, I soon arrived at the conclusion that they had equally incredible dexterity. How else could they rub and etch out such minute micro images? I'm talking about actually etching and rubbing out images on grains of sand that serve as aggregate in pottery, which by the way also proves that the pottery is over thirteen thousand years old….just from the art that's on it.

Up to now the archeological community has been concentrating on ancient man's 'megaliths'. What no one realizes is that there are hundreds of thousands of 'microliths' that tell a much clearer and vivid detailed story. The real 'greatest story ever told'. My one provenance alone has thousands of abstract artwork microliths that are telling me everything about a culture that no one even knows existed during the Ice Age, and it all came from within five miles of my home. The Mammoth People were a race of Caucasian people that lived right 'here' with the mammoth and the saber-toothed cats that preyed on the mammoth and that lived in a symbiotic relation with them. They also coexisted with lions, giraffes, sea lions, giant sloth's, horses, cattle, sheep, graylag geese, swan geese, Canada geese, grizzly and short faced bears, dire wolves, the Palomino Pony People…and did I mention...mammoth? To the Mammoth People it was just as challenging to create microlithic images as megalithic ones but with one distinct advantage... they could carry their stone age abstract artwork with them at all times and always be able to share it with their children. It was the ultimate test of your cognitive and physical abilities to produce a story or theme around many micro images that created 'scenes' on a tiny piece of stone, bone or pottery shard. That's right….I said pottery shard. Some of the greatest abstract artworks are on the pottery shards which confirm once and for all that pottery was made long before the end of the last Ice Age.

I'm getting ahead of myself; let's get back to the birds. Once I figured out what the Stone Age abstract artist was doing with the bird images I soon found them on everything small which was usually the flake knives. They were making bird images flying with their wings up or with their wings down, in other words, 'flapping'. If they were just extended straight out, you could wobble the piece like a mobile toy to make it look like they were actually flying.

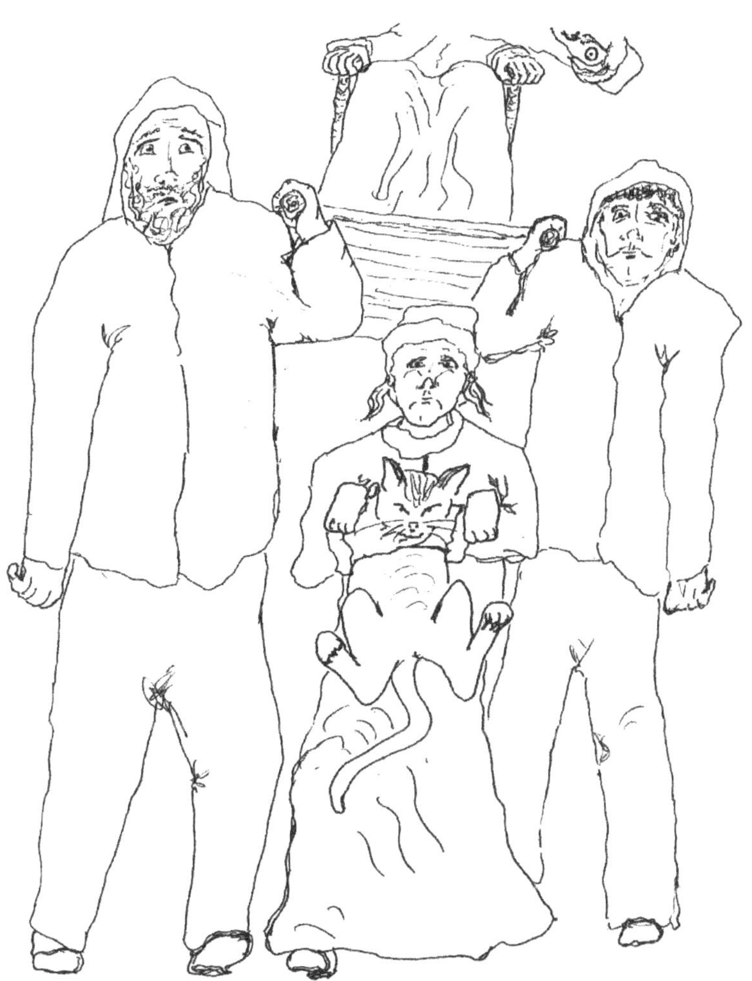

3. The upset waist high young maiden is
'madly marching' towards the other miserable weary
trekkers who have to go around her held up lead family.

Chapter Two

Optical and Cognitive Illusions

At some point when I was studying the bird images on flake knives I figured out that all that mattered to the stone age abstract artisan was that as long as he could see the perfect image of that flying bird from one distinct angle and one angle only, that's all he would need to achieve for the viewer to see its image in their 'mind's eye'. In fact, by producing the art in this way he could create many overlapping optical and cognitive illusion images around the stone. It was an essential rule to follow…. my first Stone Age microlithic abstract art 'rule'. It was so important to understand that rule because when you saw the flying bird at this one angle you knew exactly where you were seeing it from. In other words, you could hold the flint flake knife up and when you saw its perfect optical illusion of the flying bird above you, you knew exactly how high it looked and at what angle it was to the observer that was seeing it. This is also how I figured out their most important art forms. These art forms use optical and cognitive illusions to create just about all of their Stone Age microlithic abstract artworks going back to who knows how far.

Once I understood the implications of optical and cognitive illusions there was no stopping my forward progress towards discovering the Mammoth People themselves. Naturally, when you mention anything like optical and cognitive illusions, anyone would think that you yourself are delusional and that you are just seeing what you want to see. I accepted that argument early on and went about to disprove it. The very first thing that present day archeologists will have to digest, since I suspect that the majority of them are probably not intrinsically artistic, is this…..when they…or whoever is viewing the microlithic abstract art and its interpretations, gets it in their heads that it's not about how 'they' think that they should see it….rather, it's about how 'they', the Mammoth People actually saw it, then they'll start seeing the art in, on and around the stone. They (the Paleo Amerinds or Mammoth People) were figuratively seeing the art in four dimensions, not three. We look at a worked stone and our 'mind's eye' registers it as a piece of Paleo Indian worked flint. Think instead that you are looking at a three dimensional man made shape...that yes, seems to be describing something statuesque. But their abstract artwork has length, width and depth and an additional feature. There's a hidden dimension 'inside' of the translucent stone....a fourth almost mystical dimension that was as real to the Mammoth People as the other three dimensions.

All of the separate scenes that are etched and rubbed out around the whole abstract artwork combine with optical and cognitive illusions to depict a theme, an Ice Age story. Its 'pure' art which makes its abstractness all the more attractive. The Mammoth People looked at a stone and saw all of that but they also saw 'into' the stone. It was a medium in which that animal or human that they saw inside, could move through. In other words, it seems that their mystified belief system allowed them to not only see parts of animals or humans 'in' the stone but made them obligated to release their spirits by rubbing and etching them out into the most realistic image of that animal, human or bird that they could produce.

Let me give you an example. Suppose you find an image of an eagle standing in its nest. The eagle is an etched and rubbed out cognitive illusion comprised of a multitude of fossil organisms that look just like an eagle. You can't see the eagle's lower half but if you would like to see what it looks like below it all you have to do is turn it over and look up from underneath its nest, which would be like looking at the adjacent side or bottom side of the stone. There you'd see etched and rubbed out on the bottom of the stone exactly what you would see if you could look up through the bottom of the nest and see the eagles splayed out feet that are around the broken egg shells with baby eaglets around them. Another example; you see a mother duck with her wings puffed out to her sides. Her head doesn't stick up like a statue; it is etched and rubbed out bent around the stone that is an image of her body and perhaps one of the extended wings. It's wrapped around the front of the wing looking to see what's underneath it. So you turn the stone over and look up at what's under her as if you were in the ground looking up at the bottoms of her webbed feet. Once you do, you'll see the rubbed and etched out cognitive illusion images of the baby ducklings that are all around her feet and covered by her puffed out wings.

Mind you, this scenario could apply equally to a mammoth that's standing in a marsh and sucking water up that it's going to squirt into its mouth and drink or spray over itself. You would be looking at rubbed and etched out cognitive illusion images of a close-up of part of the mammoth's foot bottom and possibly the whole tip of his perfect trunk with its two flared nostrils sucking up the water. This scene would be on one side of an oval knife while the other side may be a close-up of the right side of his head that includes only his right eye, wrinkly forehead and the tip of his trunk that's spraying the white cortex water that's splashing on his wrinkly forehead. You may then move your gaze around to view the oval knife from one of the ends and slightly off to the side of it to see the etched and rubbed out optical illusion of a whole mammoth that's either walking to your left or walking to your right. In some cases you may view the end of the knife as it stands vertically in front of your gaze to see the 'walking towards you' mammoth. This art form is used quite often.

I know I took a huge leap from birds on flake knives to mammoth walking towards your gaze on large oval knives but the abstract art is consistent on all of the mediums that I looked at. I find it on heat treated flint and stone, on bone and on pottery (they especially favored pottery rim shards). I know that the skeptics will scoff because they 'know' for a fact that pottery didn't exist prior to eight thousand years before present just like all the other things that they assumed were proven on rock solid fact because of this excavation or that excavation. The fact is most archeologist work on assumptions that are supposedly verified by other archeologists. They are taught how to read the stone in a physical way. In other words, how the hammer stone was held and at what angle it struck the core to produce this beautiful fourteen centimeter long bladelett that I could shave with. Apparently no one ever scrubbed the spent blade that was worn down to six centimeters, rough on all of its edges, and was exhausted as a re-sharpened end scraper knife, because to them it was just debris or debitage. From an archaeological point of view the spent prismatic end scraper knife couldn't possibly tell you anything. Whereas a flint spear point's base could tell you the culture that produced it, which could tell you how far back in time that particular stone was being used. The spent prismatic end scraper knife that was found in a farm field with it and that was tilled over by farm implements for over a hundred and fifty years and mixed with every level of strata would be considered useless in determining anything. Yet, that spent thumb scraper was at one time a very nice 'predators bent foreleg featuring the prey its stalking' art form that was used as a knife and end scraper eating utensil. If or when it broke it was then remade into another beautiful abstract artwork just because the hunter herder microlithic abstract artist had it with him while he was passing the long hours herding or sitting in a kayak waiting for a sea lion to surface for air so he could spear it. It was the only stone he had with him so he spent countless hours peering at and into it, etching and rubbing, peering closely, rubbing and etching….for who knows how long. By the looks of some of the pieces that I've interpreted it may have taken weeks and possibly months. He would have carried that little piece of stone with him everywhere he went. To stay alert but almost motionless, he would keep his highly cognitive mind active and his body engaged for any sudden occurrence by working on his tiny piece of abstract art that was composed of many 'scenes' that combine to create a theme. Maybe the one he's working on involves him and his inexperienced son out in their white sea lion skin kayak. He's sitting in it working on this piece while his son is standing in the kayak with his spear poised to strike a Canada goose that's preoccupied with preening itself. They're dressed in white sea lion pup pelt parkas and their faces are covered in camouflage as well with only a slit for their eyes. When they're floating snow covered ice looking kayak gets within striking distance the boy throws his spear right through the neck of that unsuspecting Canada goose which makes the proud hunter herder dad see his predator son as an experienced hunter herder.

Now…I know this seems like a fictional story but it's not. This is the theme of one of the 'seemingly' spent prismatic knives that I've interpreted the abstract art on and it's just one of more than seventeen hundred artworks that have slight variations of more than twenty popular repetitive themes. You get the complete story when you don't find anymore variations of that repetitive theme on subsequent pieces that have it on them. The first image that first caught my eye was of the optical illusion flying Canada goose with its long neck and head wrapped around the front of its flying extended left wing; the prismatic knife. The gooses head is looking below it or below the ventral side of the prismatic knife, and what's below it is a reflection that's reflecting off of the bottom of its wing. When you view the ventral flat side of the prismatic knife that is the underside of its extended left wing you'll see a cognitive illusion reflection scene of the bird's eye view of the hunter herder and his son in the boat below. The hunter herder looks up to see this combined optical and cognitive illusion image, or view of the flying Canada goose. Something in the theme that you see has to see what's seeing it (another Stone Age abstract art rule). The flying goose's right wing is unseen which is how this art form presents itself. You only see one of the extended wings, the one furthest from your gaze. You are to imagine in your 'mind's eye' what the other one looks like because you already know what half of the goose's symmetry looks like, and the wing that's extended towards your gaze is the one that's always invisible. What you see instead is the rubbed out silhouette shape of the flying bird's body. This can be true of faces, heads or bodies. One art form is the left or right side view of the predator's head minus its lower jaw. You have to imagine what the lower part of the face or the 'jaw' would look like. All the abstract artist wants to do is make sure you know which predator is attacking the prey that's also in the theme and the top part of their face is usually all it takes to get their image in your 'mind's eye'.

By the end of six months of intense research with endless eureka moments and the constant state of euphoria, I was reading, or 'interpreting' the Stone Age microlithic abstract art figurative language. That's when I realized that I have all of the artifacts from a life time of searching, at least forty five years' worth, on more than twenty sites that were no more than five miles from my house (and don't fret; I had permission to look for it). For the most part I labeled all of the artifacts by site numbers starting when I was probably about fifteen years old. The earlier stuff all came off of one of two sites and you know which flint pieces those were because they're not labeled and they tended to be the biggest ones. This is because over time I picked most of it up as it surfaced leaving the smaller debris and debitage artifacts for later years, not knowing the significance that that smallest 'stuff' would play in figuring out the microlithic abstract art figurative language.

I knew that everything over thousands of years of occupation was all mixed together because of the stirring of the soil by farm implements, floods and erosion. There was no way of knowing which cultures, if there were more than one, were producing which artifacts. I had almost fifty differently designed spear and arrowhead bases and I found it hard to believe that that many different cultures lived here at one time or another. I have proven or verified that one group of inhabitants did indeed create a multitude of different spear and arrow point bases just because of the microlithic abstract art that's seen on them. These people could do anything they wanted to with stone, absolutely anything because they were at the epitome of their Stone Age existence. Why would a culture that was so creative limit itself to one particular style of spear or arrow point and their base design? They were making harpoons out of mammoth bone too because I actually found a couple of them after farm implements brought them up.

Once again I'm getting off track of the main reason for writing this book, which is to describe the Stone Age microlithic abstract art and the people who created it. I can't emphasize enough how important optical and cognitive illusions were to the Mammoth Peoples abstract art. The exploited use of these illusions not only enabled our ancestors to express themselves on a lot of available mediums, but it honed their mental cognition. It ensured their very survival by sharpening all of their senses and enabled them to be acutely 'aware' of their surroundings. By thinking inward and creating their microlithic abstract artworks using optical and cognitive illusions, they were developing the 'mind's eye' that enabled them to 'perceive' the much bigger world around them. Just think, man thought like this for hundreds of millennia and consequently still does. Just ask any magician.

The provenance of Paleo man's abstract art that I have amassed over a lifetime of searching, has taught me one sobering lesson. That is that all humans 'perceive' their surroundings differently. I am absolutely convinced that the Mammoth People honed their abstract art language skills with all of its art forms and scenes that depicted themes, as a way to unite their culture in the same way that any modern day language unites our cultures. The difference between their figurative microlithic abstract art language and our literal written one is the fact that it took so much more preconceived thought and dexterity to convey their message. They were teaching their children how to convey a message that was instantly perceived without having to say hundreds of words. And yet, it was those hundreds of descriptive words that it took to tell the story that was on and around the stone that they were showing to the child. They were storytellers and the stone was their Ice Age storybook. They definitely had their own complex literal language or I couldn't have read or interpreted those stories in my literal written one. I'm convinced that it was just as complex as our languages are today. I really think it was about sharpening all of their children's perceptive senses to the point that they were acutely aware of their surroundings that could prevent their otherwise inevitable demise which was of becoming saber-toothed cat or lion food.

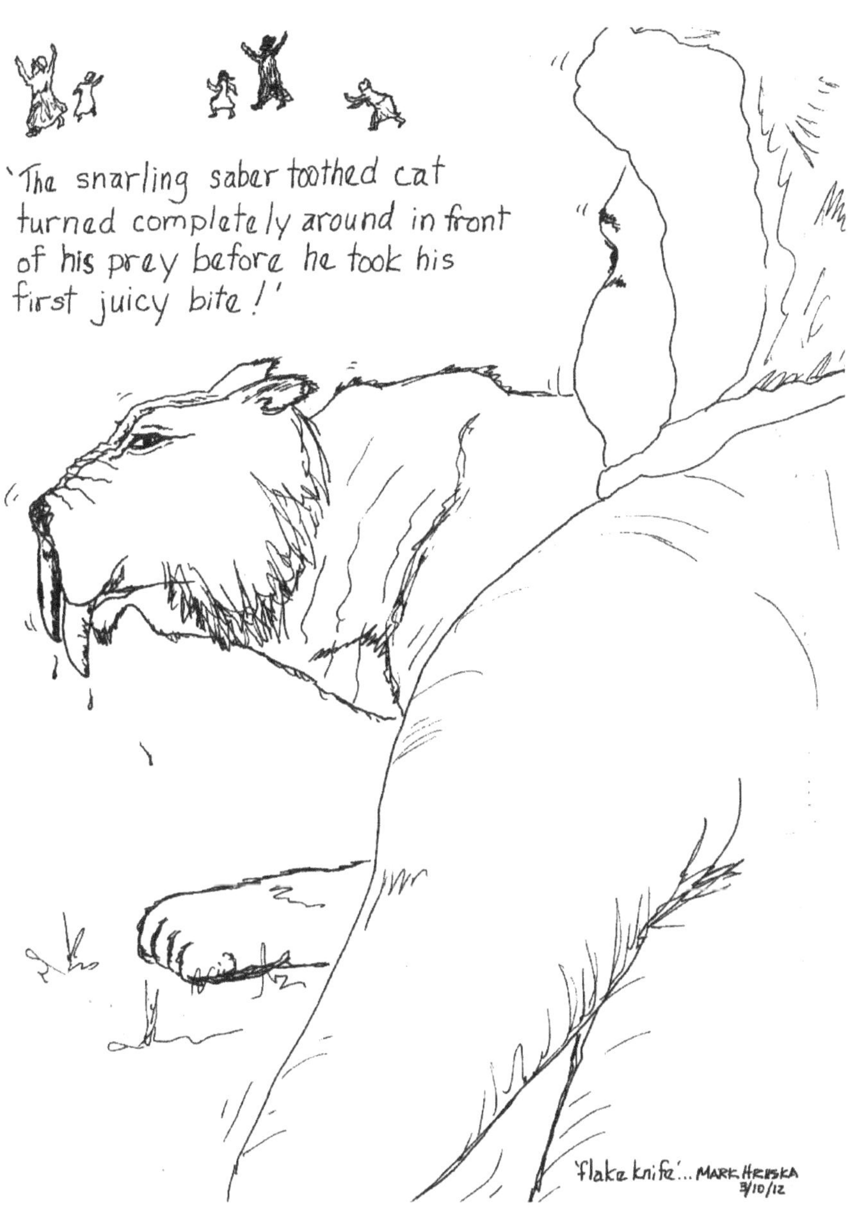

4. The hungry saber-toothed cat decided to have his own picnic snack, cornering the plumpest fleeing Mammoth People picnicker.

Chapter Three

The Description of the Mammoth Peoples Microlithic Abstract Art Language

It simply comes down to this when describing the Caucasian Mammoth Peoples microlithic abstract arts figurative language that is the latch key that unlocks the time portal to the Pleistocene....... As the interpreter of it, you are in their heads imagining the storytelling of their repetitive themes or folklore tales. You visually follow along, not by turning the pages of a two dimensional story book but by rotating the 'rotational change-up' piece that has the rubbed and etched out three dimensional combined optical and cognitive illusion close-up, almost 'statuesque' stone images, from one scene to the next. These are seen from one distinct angle and have microlithic cognitive illusion or combined optical and cognitive illusion reflection images reflecting off of them. The Mammoth People did the same thing with potsherds but they used the tiny pieces of sand aggregate that are embedded around the potsherds edges as the microlithic statuesque reflection images that reflected off of the combined optical and cognitive illusion close-up image that was the whole rubbed and etched out potsherd. These images are rubbed and etched out 'simulacrum' which is a perceived image resulting from 'pareidolia', the mind's tendency to recognize common shapes (especially faces) in random patterns. I can't just call it 'pareidolia' because there's a difference between the optical, the cognitive and the combined optical and cognitive illusion images.

Read and then reread that last paragraph until you understand it, because it's the basis of everything in this book.

There's no easy way to ease your 'mind's eye' into what I've discovered from the Mammoth People hunter herder microlithic abstract arts figurative language. Perhaps one of my biggest eureka moments came when I realized for the first time that the folks that had created the art were not red skinned Indians but in fact Caucasian....Indians. By following the 'rules' of their microlithic abstract art figurative language I realized that the red skinned people that rode palomino or 'sulphur' horses and that looked exactly like the historic plains Indians that I see in our earliest paintings of them, especially the gruff chief who wore either a single eagle feather on his head or his complete eagle feather headdress that had long trains hanging down to the ground on each side of him, were in fact predators to the Mammoth People. This is because they were portrayed on the art as they would any other predator that was attacking them such as a saber-toothed cat, lion, bear or dire wolf. It didn't take me long to figure out that the red skinned Indians were the Mammoth Peoples biggest nemesis. I also figured out that the weary Mammoth People trekked into what were the North American continents vast grassland plains that were already occupied by the Palomino Pony People, in their long mammoth caravan along with all of their domesticated animals. They were in search of a volcanic free, ice free, safe and abundant hydrologic land after having been chased out of their beloved mountainous homeland by a violently erupting volcano and its pursuing ash cloud. They endured many hardships, one being of having to trek across a vast expanse of predator ice that the violently erupting volcanoes predator ash cloud chased them out onto, after they endured the rugged volcanic mountains of their homeland.

Once I realized that it was the Mammoth Peoples microlithic abstract art that was on practically every artifact that I had found over my lifetime I became acutely aware that they were the dominant culture that lived where I have lived my entire life. The way I know that is because of the distinct differences in those two Paleo cultures' stone tools. The easiest way to explain the two lithic tool cultures that clashed in the middle of the North American continent over thirteen thousand years ago would be like this.... The Palomino Pony People (also referred to by todays archaeologists as the Clovis People) made their stone tools to be symmetrical and aesthetically pleasing to the eye, whereas the Mammoth People created their stone tools to not only be utilitarian friendly but to also incorporate scenes from one of their popular repetitive themes or folklore tales. These tales taught their children about the trials and tribulations that their ancestors experienced on their epic journey to 'here' after they were chased out of their beloved mountainous homeland by a violently erupting thunderously roaring volcano and its pursuing broiling lightning filled ash cloud.

I'd like to give you a mental picture of what it was like out here in the middle of this North American continent during the latter part of the Pleistocene. This scenario is not fictional. It was interpreted from the microlithic abstract art. Picture in your 'mind's eye' this scene...of lulling cattle and sheep in a meadow or grassland like it would have been to the south and west of the huge melting glacier here on the North American plains during the Pleistocene. The lulling cattle and sheep are being watched over by a young Caucasian man who's sitting atop a mammoth with his legs crossed. Yes, you read that right...a mammoth. The mammoth is grazing too and all of the animals just mentioned are glad to be under the watchful eye of the young man because they know he's protecting them from the saber-toothed cats, lions, bears and dire wolves that are lurking in the tall swaying prairie grass just waiting for their opportune time to strike and haul one of them off. The teenage young man is a 'herder' and while he spends his long lazy days watching over the cattle and sheep he occasionally takes out his small heat treated flint stone and his honed sharp bone awl or his limestone abrading stone and every so often, after peering intently at the stone close-up, he'll make a few rubs or etches. He's passing the many long hours of the summer day creating something that represents the things that are the most important to him. One of those things is his mammoth, which are also his beast of burden and occasionally his food supply. Also, important are his beloved cattle, sheep and graylag geese. I mean…what else is there to do on these long boring days for someone who's so intelligent? It's your turn to herd the critters and there's no way of getting out of it. It's exactly the same scenario that the Indians have in India today. They ride atop their domesticated elephants, or 'beasts of burden' while they conduct their many tasks of the day….knowing that they are safest by being atop that elephant because the elephant is the only thing that can stand up to the tigers….the man eaters. It only makes sense that during the Pleistocene man made use of the mammoth in the exact same way to protect himself from the saber-toothed cats and lions, especially in the tall prairie grass of the plains below the retreating glacier. I can see why these folks would have intentionally started grass fires just to clear away the heavy vegetation that the predator cats and dire wolves could hide in, thus giving new fresh growth for their grazing animals at the same time. It all makes perfect sense.

When I dwelt on this for a while I also realized how they got some of their butchered mammoth meat that I see on some of their abstract artworks. On the uplands of this mostly treeless North American prairie, the bull mammoth stood quite tall. He towered above the cow mammoths. He was, in most cases, a sitting duck for lightning strikes. His high domed head top would have been the first target that ground to cloud lightning would have hit. It's always the bull mammoth that got struck down by the lightning bolt that always hit the top of his head and ran down his trunk or front legs to the ground. This is why they made images of exactly that on stone, including the gouge left by the white lightning bolt on the top of his head. I doubt that they ever really had to hunt down a mammoth to survive on the 'Serengeti' type plains of Ice Age North America with all of the other animals to eat including their cattle and sheep. Since this was such a plentiful place like the 'Serengeti' of Africa there would have been frequent thunderstorms with frequent ground to cloud lightning strikes, and not many trees to strike first.

Now that I've given you a back drop of one of the environments that this stone age abstract art was produced, the other being the cold, icy and snowy environment that I'm sure was produced on the oldest art and the winter time art, I'll try to explain the abstract art 'forms' that the Mammoth People hunter herder abstract artists repeatedly used.

`Amongst all of the commotion, grandma's
yelling back at her struggling granddaughter...
..."Grab the and of my crook Sweetheart...
Grab it now!"

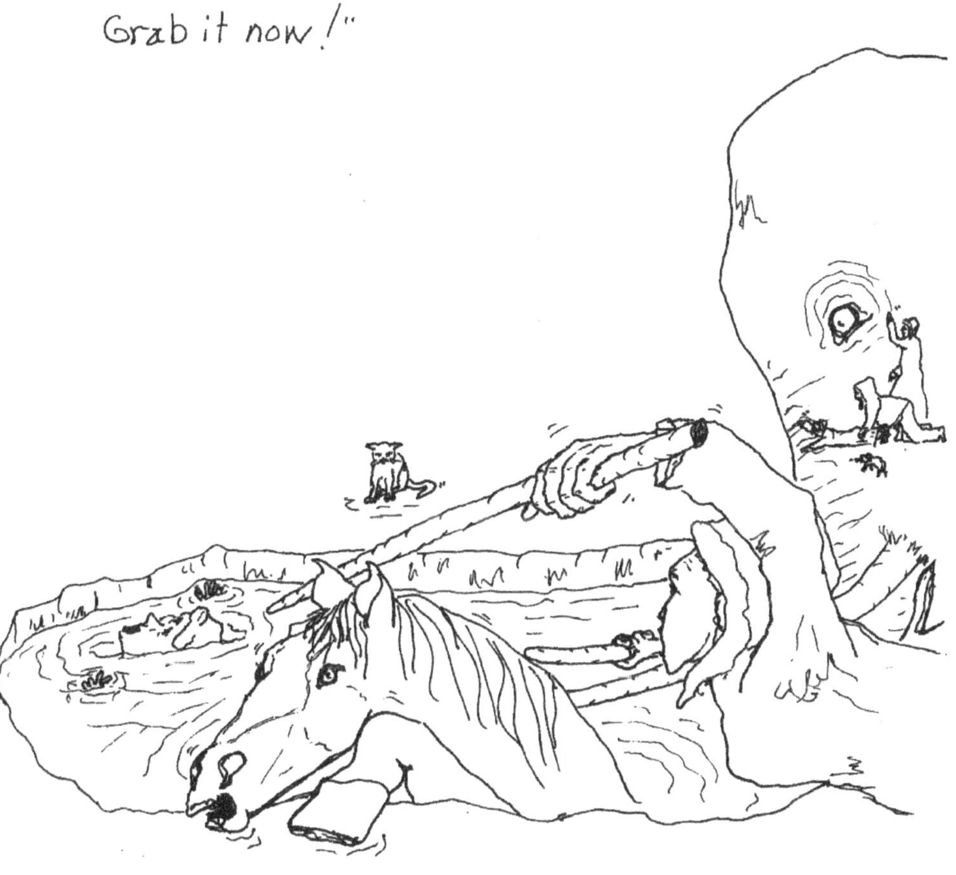

~pure microlithic abstract art'... MARK HRUSKA 4/25/12

5. The Mammoth People lead family is cooperating to
rescue the struggling fair young maiden and is reflecting
off of the left side of the kneeling nervous lead mammoth's head.

Chapter Four

Microlithic Abstract Art Forms

I had discovered many of the Mammoth Peoples' microlithic abstract art forms over that first year of research and discovery, and they have allowed me to see back in time. I named them according to exactly what I considered them to be at the moment of their discovery. They include…etched, rubbed out, optical illusions, cognitive illusions, wraparounds, close-ups and micro images or any combinations of these art forms. Then there is the cameo, which is an etched and rubbed out protruding white cortex image that's on one side of the heat treated piece of flint and that can represent anything from a birds whole body to a Caucasian humans head or face, to part of a saber-toothed cats head. Sometimes the hunter herder abstract artist rubbed down through the white cortex leaving only hints of it to create a 'snap shot' image. He did the same thing on the grey 'slip' that's on the inside side of the pottery shards. These remind me of black and white negative images which are why I called them 'snap shots'. There are three dimensional wrap around abstract art images with 'scenes' to depict a whole theme. These are artworks that go around the whole stone instead of being flat on a two dimensional canvas. The abstract artists uses a system that I call 'shafts' which can be cognitive illusions or rubbed out shafts that direct you from one scene to another even to the other side of the stone. They used 'rubbed stubs' that tell you that there is a continuation of that appendage that's missing somewhere else on the stone. An example of this would be an image of the whole side of a graylag goose minus its left foot but where it's cut off there's a rubbed out 'stub'. This tells you to look elsewhere on the stone to see it in a continuation of the image. Sometimes the 'stub' just represents the joint where you would imagine folding adjacent images together to form the complete image. An example of this would be if you were viewing the optical illusion close-up image of a seal, usually it's a sea lion, that's shown with its rear flippers that are against its lower back with a rubbed 'stub' below them. You would imagine in your 'mind's eye' that the rear flippers that were together like the flukes of a humpback whales tail, just folded over and down to complete the sea lions complete image. The same thing could be imagined with a saber-toothed cat's long top fang that would surely get broken off of the artwork if it projected out of it by itself, so it folds back under its chin.

Then there's more advance abstract art such as the 'rotational change-up' art form. This art form has rubbed or etched out cognitive illusion images or scenes that you see on one side of the piece and then you rotate the piece back, forward, clockwise or counterclockwise until that image disappears only to be replaced by the next image or scene. This art form applies to just about every piece of microlithic abstract art and is also one of the key features of the hunter herder microlithic abstract arts figurative language.

Another art form that's paramount to the microlithic abstract arts figurative language and that was pivotal for me in figuring out how it all worked is the 'opposing head' art form. 'Opposing heads' are when you see the left side of a person or animals head on the 'left' half of the face of the stone that you are viewing while you see the right side view of another person or animals head on the 'right' half. They are looking in the opposite direction and are figuratively sharing the backs of their heads. In the Mammoth People hunter herder microlithic abstract art figurative language this means that they are actually 'face to face' looking towards each other and thinking deeply of one another because they are in essence 'in' each other's heads. They can also be sharing one side of their heads by being on opposite sides of the stone. For instance, on one side of the piece you would see just the left half of a person or animals head and when you turn the piece around by bringing the front of that person or animal's face towards your gaze and then onto your right as if you wanted to see the other side or the right side of their head, what you'll see instead is the right side of the head that they're looking towards, or looking away from, but are communicating with because they're sharing one side of their heads. Like the opposite facing opposing heads, they are in effect in each other's heads thinking deeply of one another. If they are inverted to each other it almost always means that they are at odds with each other, either in a predator prey way or it could imply that they are dead to each other. Once again, remember these last two art forms because they are incorporated in every Mammoth People hunter herder microlithic abstract artwork.

When I first figured out the hunter herders microlithic abstract arts figurative language the closest thing I could compare it to in modern times is analytical and synthetic types of cubism art, but they were doing it long before Pablo Picasso, Van Gough or Gauguin and the modernist art movement. Once I figured out the basics, I found out that the Paleo microlithic abstract artisans were creating specific 'whole piece' abstract art forms such as the 'predators bent foreleg featuring the prey it's stalking' art form. This is when they took a slightly curving 's' shaped prismatic knife and shaped it into the bent foreleg of a predator which looks just like the extended foreleg of an attacking saber-toothed cat, lion, dire wolf, bear, kitty or even the mitten covered hand, boot covered foot or bare feet or hand of a human. They are what we think of as thumb scrapers or end scrapers and are always made out of prismatic knives or large bladeletts that were struck off of a core. The graver spurs around the wide scraper end of the piece are purposefully made to represent the claws on the end of the paw. All around the bent foreleg are the many scenes that depict the whole theme of the abstract artwork. The prey is almost always a microlithic cognitive illusion reflection image that's reflecting off of the underside of the swiping paw. If it's the kitty's paw, his waist high young maiden's childlike face would be reflecting off of it as he swipes towards her face because he wants her to carry him. This reminds me of something that needs to be mentioned.....all of the Mammoth Peoples abstract artwork was originally made to be the abstract artwork first and then be used as the utilitarian tool that they were aiming to use it for. If a tool broke, and because of its inherent value, they immediately made it into another abstract artwork with a repetitive theme before using it again. All of the broken end scrapers that originally were 'predators bent forelegs featuring the prey it's stalking' are made into other fantastic abstract artworks. Sometimes, they intentionally snapped them just to make a better more improved abstract artwork with a theme that centered on that image. I know for a fact that they intentionally snapped oval knives to create 'backed' knives with some fantastic themes on them.

Another art form that resembles an animal part is the 'optical illusion side view of half of an animal's head minus the lower jaw'. This is exactly what it implies and was used quite often because all you needed to see is the side of the animals head whether it's the predator or the prey, and you can tell what it is. Even if that upper part of the animal or human's optical illusion head is split in half down the middle of its face and you're only seeing the top quadrant of one side of their face, you can still tell what animal or human that you're looking at. You really don't need the lower jaw to get the image in your 'mind's eye'. Furthermore, in cases where it's the saber-toothed cat with his ear pinned back and an etched out squinting tiger like eye, all you need to see to complete a realistic image of one side of his head would be to see his long saber fang. Well…to accommodate you with that image, the hunter herder abstract artist will show either an etched out image or a cognitive illusion image of the saber fang for that side of the saber toothed cats face under its maxilla or upper jaw. In other words, if you tip his snout or muzzle back and look at where the roof of his mouth should be you'll see the saber fang that is supposed to fold out and snap into place completing his realistic image in your 'mind's eye'. This can apply equally to mammoths that don't have their trunks or tusks as part of their close-up cognitive or optical illusion images. Somewhere else on the piece you'll see perhaps a perfect long curving white cognitive illusion tusk that would fit on it perfectly and it will be proportional to its head's dimensions. In cases with tusks I've seen many examples where there's a rubbed out polished 'stub' where the tusk is supposed to attach.

Another art form is the use of 'tracks'. To give an example of this microlithic abstract art form, think of a 'predators bent foreleg featuring the prey it's stalking' end scraper. The whole thing represents the predator's swiping left or right extended front foreleg and paw. Well….in some cases the hunter herder abstract artist produced the whole piece around that kind of predators tracks that he saw 'in' the stone on the flat ventral side of the piece and they would be on the middle of the underside of that predators paw. In other words, the animals track is in the middle of the inside of its own paw. This only goes to show that they could work and shape a stone around a microlithic cognitive illusion image with the ease that we would shape molding clay.

The Mammoth People were all about mammoth, saber-toothed cats and lions with lesser degrees of their sheep, cattle, cats and dogs. Consequently much of their art is associated with the mammoth form or shape. Some of their flint tools that I've found, I discovered were actually a replication of part of the mammoth's anatomy. For instance, the 'T' shaped drills that really aren't drills at all, represent the mammoths long wavy trunk and the area of the front of its face that encompasses its eyebrow ridges. They were probably used as hair pins that held the women's rolled up pigtails to the side of their heads in a round bun over their ears. Try to picture princess Leia on 'Star Wars'. I'm convinced they did this on purpose to help protect their heads in case a saber-toothed cat ambushed them because the saber-toothed cats always went for their heads. The rolled up hair would be like a wound up woven rope on the sides of their heads that would give some protection. I have their images with their hair up like this many times and it's best seen on the pottery shard abstract artworks.

Another art form that is used as a tool or eating utensil is the oval shaped end scrapers that represent the forehead and upper trunk area of a mammoth. Some end scrapers represent side views of the whole mammoths head including the ear and trunk. The wrinkly trunk is actually etched or rubbed out wrapped along the side of the scraper edge as if it were spraying water on its head, or it's bent under as if it's putting water directly in its mouth.

Another art form is the 'walking mammoth'. It can be on flint knife scrapers, stone or pottery. It can be large or small and they usually show the mammoth either walking towards you or to your right or left. The 'walking towards you' mammoth is pretty common and many times the lead hunter herders head is superimposed on the upper middle and to the left of his trunk as he leads the mammoth by walking slightly in front and to the left of its left eye. The most common image of the 'walking towards you' mammoth is of when you see the whole front of its head including its long trunk. Some are made from baked rock which proves that they were doing that that long ago. They are usually featured with the mammoth's long wavy trunk swinging to its right side, out of the way of its forward stepping left front foot.

Then there's the 'mammoth heads' art form. These can be made from flint or stone. The stone ones come in many shapes and they are all usually made from brown, greenish or grayish stone that has the texture, including the wrinkles of the mammoth's skin. For instance, they would take a fractured stone and work it so that it would look like the close-up view of a mammoth's forehead with an eye. Or have the top of the domed head top with an ear, etc. Many of these representations will also feature a rams head somewhere else on the stone. This mammoth/ram feature or mammoth/bull feature has turned up quite often and I knew that it had something to do with the importance of all three of these domesticated animals to the Mammoth People. Many times I found the mammoth, the ox and the rams head images on the same piece which usually represents how they were walking in the Mammoth People mammoth caravan. They were usually walking abreast of each other with the ox to the right of the mammoths head and the ram walking to the left of the mammoths head. I later came to find out that the ox was actually the domestic milk cow that carried the infant who was strapped to a backboard that was slung over her left shoulder. By trekking in this manner, mom who was walking between the mammoth and the domestic milk cow could be face to face with her infant and they both had some defense against predators as they trekked in their Mammoth People mammoth caravan to 'here'.

Another art form is the large hand held stone mammoth heads that are all made in the exact same shape and involve a lightning bolt that's hitting the top of their heads and running down the side of them. Sometimes they even show a chunk missing from the top of the head where the lightning bolt strikes. All I know is that this was an important representation for them and what I'm deriving from it is that since many of these mammoth heads are large pounding stones, they want to 'strike' whatever they're pounding them against, with the same intensity as lightning striking the head of the mammoth. Or it simply represented the lightning that's reflecting off of the mammoth as it treks over the rugged mountains during the middle of the Pleistocene night when they or their ancestors were fleeing the violently erupting volcano and its broiling ash cloud that chased them out of their beloved mountainous homeland. The same goes for the smaller ones that are knives. They want to slice that meat with the same intensity as a striking lightning bolt.

The 'cut off mammoth ear' is another mammoth art form. It's usually a 'backed' knife that features rats chewing on the jagged edged ear that was sliced off by marauding saber-toothed cats. The rubbed flat edge is where the saber fangs sliced it off after which it fell to the ground somewhere along the chase route and rats are eating it. When you see it you automatically know that it represents one of the Mammoth People mammoth caravan themes where marauding saber-toothed cats attacked them...much like modern day tigers would attack a running elephant in India.

Another art form is when one side of a prismatic knife, usually the concave ventral side, is made to look like an animal that's 'lying down' or lulling. Their heads are wrapped around the knife like the birds heads and necks do. Usually these are cattle, sheep or in one instance, a palomino stallion.

One of these laying down animal art forms exclusively represents the 'submissive ewe'. This is when you see the fleecy white ewe with her chin flat on the ground as if she's sleeping. Well…she's not. This is usually how a sheep looks when a predator attacks them by jumping on top of their back and biting the nape of their neck. They simply lay their heads chin on the ground and submit because they know that they don't stand a Pleistocene chance. The Mammoth People used this image a lot especially when someone was getting killed by an attacking predator. I eventually figured out that the submissive ewe represented the 'flying submissive ewe spirit' because she's shown with big white feathery flapping bird wings and her image is usually shown with her chin lying on the head of the dying Mammoth People persons head, and many times she's shown with her wings just like you would see a goose flying only the submissive ewe spirit was flying or gliding in over the site of where a Mammoth People person was about to expire with the tragic scenes of the repetitive theme reflecting off below her. Usually the whole piece is one of her extended wings with her submissive ewe head and neck wrapped around the edge of it. Her body is on the 'stub' end of the piece with the visible wing extended out from the other side of it. Much of the theme will be reflecting off of the underside of her wing but many of the scenes of the repetitive theme or 'folklore tale' could be seen reflecting off of any part of her, seen from one distinct angle. When you see her image you know for sure that one of the Mammoth People or one of their domestic animals which were almost like family members, were dying and she's swooping down to suck up their last exhaled dying breath from their opened mouth which is their spirit. She then takes it into the heavens to be with their deceased ancestors, which brings up the next art form……

The cremation or funeral pyre art form is most prevalent on potsherd rim pieces and is also on some of the flint pieces that have the color blue, which is a very rare color in heat treated flint or any stone for that matter that is found in this area of the planet. The potsherd rim piece is made to look just like the side view of a funeral pyre that has the body or what's left of the victim that was chewed up by one of the Ice Age predators, lying on top of it. In many cases it could be made out of a fairly small piece of potsherd rim because all that they were cremating was what was left of the victim which was usually their head! You'll almost always see the submissive ewe spirit associated with these abstract artworks. She's seen flying, gliding or lying in wait until the dying victim expires. This also shows that the Mammoth People were a docile people and most likely worshiped to more of a pantheist type of religion. I could have easily named this Caucasian hunter herder culture the 'Submissive Ewe Spirit People' much like we call Jesus followers Christians and that's because the flying submissive ewe spirit seems to be present in all of their repetitive themes or folklore tales that involve death, birth and weddings. If she isn't gliding down to suck up their dying last exhaled breaths or spirits, she's gliding down to deliver a blessing such as the unity blessing that she blows into the bride and grooms mouths as they recite the response to the magistrate's incantation while his raised hands are placed over the couples' heads.

Another abstract art form that I've identified is when the hunter herder microlithic abstract artist uses the 'all seeing' eye of a grouse or quail's head. It usually takes place on a stone that's shaped like the head of a quail or grouse. The bird sees a 'scene' that describes the theme of the artwork and its reflecting off of that all seeing eye, much like the 'predators bent foreleg that features the prey it's stalking' art form that has the prey that it's stalking reflecting off of the underside of its 'swiping' paw. On one particular piece that had this art form the birds head and 'all seeing' eye have the reflections of an attack, killing and eating of a giraffe by three to five lionesses. Late in my research I figured out that the giraffes were domesticated and actually travelled to 'here' with the Mammoth People in their long mammoth caravan. In fact, I interpreted one piece that had the 'volcanic mass exodus' folklore tale on it and in it a pair of giraffes was walking abreast of each other amongst the ranks of other miserable weary trekkers, and the whole artwork was created around them.

The preening goose or gander is another common art form. It's much like the 'lying down animal' and it usually shows the goose or the vain gander preening under one of their wings or preening their tail and not paying any attention to possible predators. I found this to be the case in one of the 'inexperienced son' repetitive hunting themes where the goose was preening her tail feathers to show that she was preoccupied and not paying attention to her surroundings while the inexperienced young lad snuck up on her and speared her, which taught the Mammoth People children to never let their guards down, as if they had eyes in the backs of their heads. The optical illusion close-up image of the preening goose drew you into the storyline of that folklore tale.

The 'human mating stone' would have to be considered another abstract art form. I know it sounds more like a theme but it always has the same imagery on it. It's always a woman's head and the stub of her neck. She's always shown with her mouth wide opened. She has a pointy perky nose and has her head arched back with long flowing hair seemingly being blown back behind her. Viewed upright, she appears to be singing and at first reminds you of the singing sirens of Greek mythology but in fact, she is lying down on her back and she is in the throes of climaxing during intercourse, yes, it's real. You are to view her head in a supine position with her hair falling back behind her. The mating stone art form also features the scenes of mating animals, maybe all of the ones that were important to the Mammoth People because reproduction was paramount on their minds, especially the oversexed teenage young lad hunter herders. One of the artworks even has a lunar calendar on it showing the different phases of the moon to show when the baby would be born.

I think that one of the oldest Mammoth People hunter herder microlithic abstract art forms is one in which the optical illusion image of the predator and prey are shown nose tip to nose tip. A few of them feature the theme with the orca and the sea lion which means that whoever created these pieces had been out to sea observing them from their kayak, pretty shocking considering that I picked the artwork up out of a tilled field in the center of the North American continent. This means that they had to travel to the center of this continent in one lifetime, possibly even from Europe. This can be proven because I have many artworks with the images of the black Scottish Terrier dog on them, so much for the dog descending from the wolf in the last ten thousand years. The Scottish Terrier was here over thirteen thousand years ago and it probably came from the area that is now the highlands of Scotland, meaning that the Mammoth People came from somewhere near the present day British Isles. Later on I interpreted many pieces with the Bloodhound dog on it. The Bloodhound would have been a great hunting dog but was used mainly to help herd the cattle and mammoth while the Scottic was more of a home watch dog and rat catcher, and was a favorite of grandma or the waist high young lad. I have many artworks that show the Scottie with the Mammoth People when they were fleeing a violently erupting volcano. On some pieces I've seen twin peaks where the one to the right is erupting with the cloud of ash streaming over the Mammoth People mammoth caravan and they're trekking away from its anvil that appears to be an angry male lion that's about to pounce on them with lightning coming out of his head. This leads me to believe that they headed west from somewhere with the same environment that Kamchatka has to this day. They were chased out of their beloved mountainous and volcanic homeland by the violently erupting volcano out onto and along the edge of the Pacific ice sheet that had a deep dark icy cold abyss below it. They were simply fleeing the erupting volcano that drove them out of their homeland. This is what I was seeing on those earliest interpreted pieces that also usually tended to be the largest pieces. The rapid education was unceasing as I interpreted pieces nonstop and I soon found out much more that included volcanoes. Did I mention that the mammoth pulled sleds? That reminds me of the next art form…..

The potsherd piece that's shaped like a sled when you view it one way, but when you invert it, it morphs into the mammoth that's pulling it. She's either pulling it to your left or to your right. A pulling mammoth looks different than a regular walking mammoth because she always has one of her hind legs extended back as if she's moving at a fairly fast gait, as if running. When you turn the piece upside down the extended back leg becomes the front of the sled that slants up and forward. Grandma is usually in the sled with her ewe and lambs and there's usually a saber-toothed cat closing in on the back of the sled. Grandma is usually hollering at the lead hunter herder which is most likely her son, to run because she's first in line when the big cats catch them and clamber over the back of the sled.

Another art form that I've learned about is when a sharp angled heat treated stone that has two or more rubbed flat adjacent sides form a honed sharp straight knife edge. I knew that they were something special that the Mammoth People hunter herder microlithic abstract artist created and that the piece is not just a knife. I call these pieces 'geometric' microlithic abstract art forms. One of the interpretations that I did had two flat sides that were at a shallow angle to each other forming a knife edge but in the interpretation of the piece, the honed sharp knife edge, along with the rest of the whole piece viewed from one specific angle was the steep gable roofed cottage that the sorceress and her three chanting assistants were conducting the exorcism ceremony on unconscious grandpa in. These pieces also tend to have outstanding combined optical and cognitive illusion close-up images on them even though they seem to be simple shapes. What creates the illusions are the partially worked jagged edges of the piece that simply seem to be the fractured edges of the heat treated stone that cracked and broke apart along it's crazed lines. Since you assume that that's what happened to the heat treated stone you tend to not look at it closer.

I interpreted a lot of the heat treated stone pieces that were used as knife scraper eating utensils. And although many of them fall under the geometric microlithic abstract art form, there's another style that I've taken for granted and just assumed would be understood. I need to specifically state its art form, and that is the one of the fractured heat treated stones that has the 'pecked out imagery' on the fractured inside side of the stone. Some of these pecked out images are on almost flat surfaces and you will only be able to see them from one specific angle much like the rest of the Mammoth People hunter herder microlithic abstract art. The microlithic abstract artist utilizes the jagged edges that are around the fractured heat treated stone that most likely fractured along the crazed lines and he uses them to create the silhouettes of the faces of the characters in their repetitive themes. Those jagged edges make perfect graver spurs and scraper edges. So a Mammoth People child could be using one of the jagged edges as a graver spur but isn't thinking about it as a graver spur at all. They're thinking instead of it as either irate grandma's, crotchety grandma's or cursing grandpa's pointy noses or pointy chins that are scraping the meat off of the bone as they eat. They're constantly being reminded of the trials and tribulations that their ancestors endured in order to get to 'here'.... which was an awesome place to live free of volcanoes, ash clouds, predator ice with a deep dark icy cold abyss below it and countless other disasters like glacial ice dam ruptures that caused epic deluge floods. Albeit, they did adapt some new nemesis such as lions, saber-toothed cats and the worst one....the Palomino Pony People.....

I'd like to revisit one of the most important art forms here near the end of their descriptions so that it leaves the longest lasting impression on your 'mind's eye'. That is the 'opposing heads' art form. Many times it's Mammoth People's heads and faces that you see opposing each other and they both have hoods on. Actually, I find many more of them with bonnets on because most of the repetitive themes involve grandma and her fair young maiden or waist high young maiden granddaughter.

As mentioned earlier, opposing heads can also be shown when there's the left or right side of a heads face etched out on one side of the stone but on the other side there's a different face and they share the same nose and front of their faces that are on the edge of the piece. They're still considered opposing heads sharing one side of their heads because one is a left side view and the other is a right side view and they could be imagined face to face or nose to nose.

Another example is when you simply invert the face that's etched out on the edge of the piece and it becomes or 'morphs' into the face of another character. They're upside down from each other but they're still considered opposing heads, but ones that are at 'odds' with each other. An example of this is when you have the lead hunter herder's hood covered head's face pointing to your left. You're seeing the left side of his hood covered head and bearded face. When you turn him upside down he becomes or morphs into the right side view of his inexperienced son's hood covered head and pug nosed childlike face that he took sea lion pup hunting.

One of the most awe-inspiring art forms that I discovered late in the deciphering of the Mammoth People hunter herder microlithic abstract art figurative language is that of the microlithic fine etching near the edge of the stone that shows one side view of the characters of the theme as 'silhouette images superimposed to the side of each other in succession to give a side view of them standing abreast of each other'. An example would be; as if they were running abreast of each other out ahead of a windblown prairie fire and you were also in that line looking to your left or right at the rest of them all fleeing for their lives as you ran for your own life with them.

That covers most of the art forms and when you combine them with the microlithic abstract art rules which we'll cover in the next chapter, a novice should be able to read and interpret their own pieces of Paleolithic microlithic abstract art. Using the deciphered Paleo Amerind microlithic abstract art figurative language will eventually lead to the answers archeologically, artistically and most importantly anthropologically, to so many of the questions concerning Paleolithic man on this North American continent near the end of the Pleistocen.

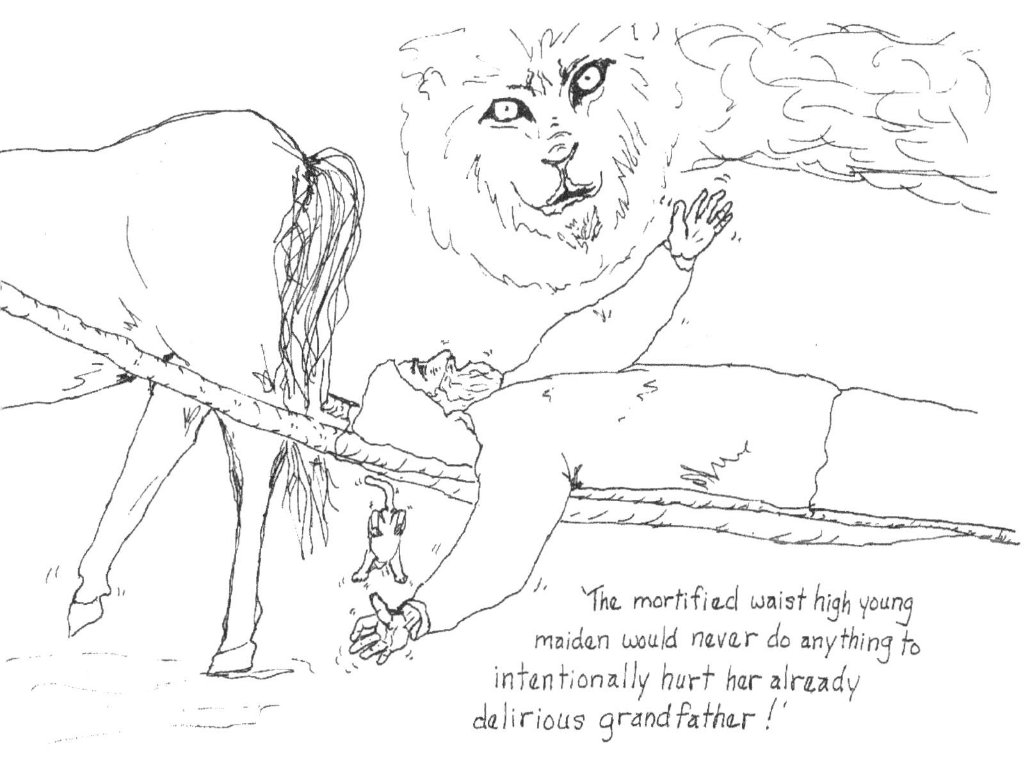

6. The waist high young maiden's frightened
kitty has just scratched grandpa's face making him more
delirious than he already was because he thought that he was
seeing the roaring male lion volcanic ash cloud that close up.

Chapter Five

Microlithic Abstract Art Rules

We'll be able to find the answers to so many questions that are raised about the Mammoth Peoples travels from their microlithic abstract artworks alone because you will no longer have to dig up a mammoth along with their artworks embedded in it, nor will you have to sift down through layer after layer of dirt to verify if it's thirteen thousand years old or older strata that the microlithic abstract artwork was found in. The Mammoth Peoples hunter herder microlithic abstract arts figurative language will stand on its own and reveal who created the pieces and how long ago they did simply by their likenesses and those of Ice Age predators that are on them, even if they've been interred in a plowed farm field in the middle of the Corn Belt and haven't seen the light of day for over thirteen millennia. So here is the expanded set of 'rules' that I've come up with as I deciphered the microlithic abstract arts figurative language. These rules consistently complement the art forms to create the microlithic abstract art figurative language. Keep in mind that all of these rules were figured out during many Eureka moments of discovery and were established before I found any imagery of the Mammoth People themselves on their own microlithic abstract art which gives these rules credence since the art rules combined with the art forms led me to their very discovery.

Rule one: Three dimensional abstract artworks must show something that clarifies the theme on every side of the piece once you find art on any one side, even on an edge if it's rubbed, which technically makes it another side.

Rule two: The color and texture of the piece of stone has a great deal to do with the animal that the work of art is going to portray. The hunter herder microlithic abstract artist is obligated to make it look as real as possible. Color and texture are extremely important so if the stone is grey you would concentrate first on the more obvious like sea lions, mammoth etc. Tan and brown would suggest saber-toothed cats or lions. Flecked grey and white is almost always sheep's fleecy wool....you get the point.

Rule three: The larger the piece of stone the bigger the animal that's usually portrayed on it.

Rule four: If there is a rubbed out nose, trunk or snout end with two nostril dots either etched out or as cognitive illusions, then there's an animal that goes with it somewhere on the stone, usually on an adjacent side of the stone.

Rule five: If there's a rubbed out 'stub' there must be a continuation of it somewhere else on the stone unless it's the stub of 'opposing heads' necks.

Rule six: When the hunter herder microlithic abstract artist continue a 'stub' somewhere else on the piece, it has to have the same color or texture as the original 'stub', but sometimes a 'stub' just means to look for a whole other image of the same thing. That same thing could include a whole animal image as long as it contains the continuation 'stub' piece.

Rule seven: Sometimes, instead of a 'stub', the hunter herder abstract artist used a rubbed out 'shaft' that would lead directly to where the artwork continued, for instance, to another side of the stone. For example, they may etch and rub out a bovine bull's face and head on one side of the piece and directly above his head over to the other side of the stone, connected by the shaft would be the perfect horn pointing forward in just the right direction. It would be as if you could elevate it down right on top of the bull's head.

Rule eight: White translucent inclusions and sparkly quartz crystalline inclusions were very desirable and valuable to the hunter herder abstract artist, almost like diamonds are to us. No joking. So they tended to make them into the things most precious to them like eyes or crying eyes, egg holes and or mating holes because reproduction was paramount to them. You'll also see tusks, and trunk tips made out of crystalline inclusions or translucent whitish flint that can also represents frothy foam, water or just plain.....snot.

Rule nine: Mating holes always tend to be portrayed as square whether they're on a goose or on a mammoth. So if you find a mating theme on a 'wrap around' flying goose wing and the mating hole is square there's an excellent chance that it was produced during the Pleistocene.

Rule ten: Family and mating were powerful themes and often used together on the same artwork piece, in other words you could have a whole 'loving' sheep family theme on one oval knife. It could include images of the ram, ewe and lamb, images of the ram 'riding' the ewe and even images of the ram's erect penis.

Rule eleven: If there's a protrusion on the forehead of one of the Paleo abstract art images then there is definitely another image somewhere else on the stone, if not right there. More than likely it's another head image.....as in 'opposing heads' and the protrusion is a microlithic reflection image of the other opposing head that they're face to face with.

Rule twelve: When the artist makes a cutoff point of arms, legs, necks, or whatever, as jagged rubbed edges he does it to show that it's just a discontinuation of the scene and not part of the scene as in being bit off. The exception is the rubbed flat edge that's on the cut off mammoth ear art form that is usually being chewed on by rats. Those are almost always rubbed flat to represent the edge that the saber-toothed cat sliced off and they are the flat edge of the backed knife which is the rest of the ear because it's used to push against to apply finger pressure to the opposite cutting edge of the piece which is the honed sharp knife edge or outside edge of the ear.

Rule thirteen: When the Ice Age artist wants to show motion or progression such as the 'flicking tail' of a mating lioness he usually shows multiple images of the tail. The artist can do the same thing with the head of a saber-toothed cat by producing several images of its head that get progressively bigger as if it's advancing forward or towards your gaze because it's getting closer and closer to the prey that it's attacking and that you are seeing through the horrified eyes of. Another example would be that you would see several overlapping images of a cow's head because she's licking off the afterbirth that's on her newborn calf's head. These motion scenes are 'proto-cinema' scenes and they all give you the sense of movement.

Rule fourteen: If the hunter herder abstract artist didn't have room to show an image, he just made the invisible outline of part of its shape. For instance, the young Mammoth People mother could be sitting side saddle atop a mammoth. You may see her whole body but none of the mammoth that she's sitting on. You know she's sitting on the mammoth because of the curved invisible outline of the arching back of the mammoth that's underneath her and making an impression against the underside of her. It's the 'invisible outline' rule. Another example would be if you see the whole piece as the combined optical and cognitive illusion close-up image of the left side view of the lead hunter herder's head that has a rubbed out crescent shaped concave edge exactly where the top of his left shoulder would be. That rubbed out concave edge 'is' the invisible top edge of his left shoulder which gives you a good idea of what position he is in by the relationship that his head has with the position of the top of his invisible left shoulder. It could indicate that he's standing erect like he is when he's face to face with the gruff chief or it could indicate that he is bent over down on his knees and holding down on the back of grandma's legs as she stretches out over the hole in the predator ice and reaches for their fair young maiden who's struggling to keep her head above the icy cold churning ocean water. The struggling fair young maidens head could be shown as an 'opposing head' to him because they're looking towards each other, and she could be portrayed with her face looking skyward as she struggles to keep her chin above the icy cold water. The hunter herder microlithic abstract artist does that by rubbing out the edge of the piece that is the part that encompasses the right side of her desperate looking childlike face, to be the invisible outline of the top of the sea water or the 'waterline' that she's trying to keep her chin above.

Rule fifteen: This Mammoth People hunter herder microlithic abstract art 'rule' seems more like a 'technique'. I've seen it used many times now, especially on the repetitive theme of the 'volcanic mass exodus'. I found it used on a different repetitive theme that's of the Mammoth People springtime picnic that's being raided by a pair of rogue male lions and I absolutely have to record it. On this particular piece there's a rubbed out microlithic cognitive illusion image of the front left side view of the screaming waist high young maiden on the left side of her screaming mothers combined optical and cognitive illusion close-up images nose and mouth. She's clearly not a reflection and you are seeing her as if you were looking past the front of her screaming mothers head's face, the way that the flying submissive ewe spirit would see both of them as she glides in to suck up their last exhaled breaths...or spirits. Likewise, in the 'volcanic mass exodus' repetitive theme, the lead hunter herder or 'dad' is always portrayed as crotchety grandma's front right porter and he's standing abreast to the right of his teenage young lad son who is always the front left porter. You'll see a combined optical and cognitive illusion close-up image of the compassionate teenage young lad's face that's being seen by his sobbing little sister who's standing in front of him and looking up towards his compassionate face. Then you'll see a microlithic cognitive illusion image of the perfect left side view of their dad's head and stern looking face on the left side of the nose of the disgusted teenage young lads combined optical and cognitive illusion close-up image. The microlithic cognitive illusion smaller image of dad isn't a reflection image of him. You are actually seeing him as he looks when you look past the front of the disgusted teenagers face the way that the sobbing waist high young maiden would see him. This is a way that the hunter herder microlithic abstract artist can convey the figurative message that the sobbing waist high young maiden sees her compassionate big brother as a 'bigger man' than her stern looking dad who is portrayed as a smaller further away image. She's reflecting off of the front left side of her compassionate big brother's chest looking towards her stern faced dad. She's looking past her closer up 'big man' brother's face to see her...'smaller man' stern dad's further away face.

Rule sixteen: Sometimes, the optical illusion or combined optical and cognitive illusion close-up images of a Mammoth People person's face is the close-up of the microlithic cognitive illusion image that's somewhere on the side of their head or face. It's not always a reflection image. Other times, when you see a reflection image of someone near the edge of the combined optical and cognitive illusion close-up images face, you are actually seeing the further away image of that person that's on the other side of them and further away as if the close-up person is shouting or looking towards that further away person as described in rule fifteen.

Rule seventeen: The different sized crescent shaped rubs that are on the edges of the flint microlithic abstract artworks are intentionally created to have the ends of your thumb or index finger to fit into in order to position the piece for a particular image or scene as you hold it, usually with your left hand's fingers...just as a straight edge or adjacent straight edges that are at ninety degrees to each other can set you up for an image or scene by placing one of the straight edges at the bottom of the piece horizontal to your gaze while the other straight edge is vertical to your gaze. If there's only one straight edge on the piece, place it at the bottom horizontal to your gaze to set you up for the first scene. Sometimes you may have to position the piece so that that straight edge is to your lower left or lower right at a forty five degree angle to your gaze. An example of this would be when you see the combined optical and cognitive illusion close-up image of the left side view of the struggling fair young maiden's head with her face looking skyward because the straight edge of the piece is encompassing the left side of her face. That's because the straight edge that may also appear to be jagged, represents the invisible outline of the waterline that the fair young maiden is struggling to keep her chin above. If you invert her head it may morph into the inverted 'opposing head' to her of her thrashing horse. They would be opposing heads that are at 'odds' with each other because they are sharing the backs of their inverted heads meaning that they are 'in' each other's inverted heads thinking deeply of one another during the Pleistocene tragedy. The reason that they're inverted or at odds with each other is because they're both vying for room in the hole in the predator ice which gives the thrashing horse the upper hand or hoof because his flailing front feet's hooves could easily kick the struggling fair young maiden in her bonnet covered head rendering her unconscious and sending her sinking into the dark icy cold abyss.... Another example of the forty five degree angled straight edge is when it's used to create the invisible outline of delirious grandpa's left or right travois pole.

In short, the crescent shaped rubs helped the Mammoth People children position their knife scraper eating utensil storytelling tool so that they themselves could read and recite the popular folklore tales, perhaps while they also used one of those crescent shaped rubs as a 'shaft scraper' to scrape the meat off of a cooked goose bone...

Rule eighteen: I saved this one for last because it's the most important Mammoth People microlithic abstract art rule. If you see the image of a human or animal with an eye, that eye is seeing one of the images or scenes that are seeing it. Every image or scene that you see on the abstract artwork whether it's on stone, potsherds or bone, is being seen by one of the characters that are portrayed in the theme. For example, if there's a bird's eye view of the den site where the saber-toothed cats and their cubs are eating their kill of mammoth...or lead hunter herder, then there has to be the image of the bird's head and the eye that's in it as the bird fly's over, being seen by one of the cat's eyes. It could even be seen by one of the decapitated heads that has a dead wide opened eye that's looking skyward at the soaring bird above. It's most likely the eye of a teratornis vulture that swoops down close. In one interpretation it was the eye of the giraffe looking over the tree tops down on the den site of the lions that were eating another giraffe that they killed. I was looking for a bird when all along it was the tall long necked giraffe that had the bird's eye view.

Another example: If there's the optical illusion close-up image of the left side view of the mammoths head with her 'all seeing' left eye, she's most likely being seen that close to her left eye by the lead hunter herder's hood covered heads right eye. When the lead hunter herder turns his head to the right and looks slightly behind and above his right shoulder, he'll be looking into the left eye of the lead mammoth which in turn sees his right eye to her left and slightly ahead and below her.

Rule nineteen: When you think you've figured out or have completely interpreted one of the Mammoth People hunter herder's microlithic abstract artworks.......think again....there's always more.

I ended the Mammoth People hunter herder abstract art rules with the 'every eye sees another eye' rule so that I could explain the basis of all of the Mammoth People abstract art repetitive themes. That is that all of the Mammoth People hunter herder microlithic abstract arts repetitive themes center on the fact that everything you see is being viewed by another character in the theme, which is being composed of several scenes. Generally this is the way it all plays out.....Let's assume that you're viewing a Mammoth People mammoth caravan microlithic abstract artwork. As often is the case with these repetitive themes, a saber-toothed cat is attacking the various members of the caravan. This could be the mammoth, the lead hunter herder, his wife, the domestic milk cow or the infant that's strapped to a backboard and slung over her left shoulder, and let's not forget the black faced ram that's usually walking to the left of the lead hunter herder, or it could be attacking grandma who's riding in the sled that's being pulled by the mammoth instead of sitting on her special armchair atop its back. She's tending her ewe and lambs but usually just a pair of lambs in the mammoth pulled sled. However the hunter herder microlithic abstract artist wants to make his story go, he'll always show it happening as if you were seeing it through the eyes of the character that's witnessing it, even if he or she is dead or was killed and their uneaten head's glassy eye is still opened. Everything you see is witnessed through the eyes of one of the characters, dead or alive. Several of these scenes combine to create the repetitive theme of the artwork....the folklore tale.

This is how one of their common themes usually plays out, and I know that you already just finished reading part of it, but it doesn't hurt to go over it again…. The mammoth's 'all seeing' left eye looks down and slightly in front of her to see the close-up image of the top and slightly rear right side view of the lead hunter herder's hood covered head. When the lead hunter herder turns to his right and looks slightly behind and up over his right shoulder he sees the close-up image of the left side view of the mammoths head including her 'all seeing' left eye. When the mammoth looks to her right with her 'all seeing' right eye, she's looking down on the close-up of the left side view of the domestic milk cow's horned or dehorned head and she also sees the front of the infant's face that's sticking up higher than the domestic milk cow's left shoulder that the infant's backboard carrier is slung over. She sees the domestic milk cow's left eye and both of the infant's eyes. They in turn can see her 'all seeing' right eye and the close-up image of the right side view of her head. When the lead hunter herder turns to his right he can look past the front of the lead mammoth's head to see the front left side view of the domestic milk cow's head, neck and left shoulder with his infant slung over her left shoulder. Consequently their eyes can also see him, giving great comfort to the infant that sees his dad so close. More importantly, dad can get to his infant if the saber-toothed cats that are lurking in the tall swaying prairie grass decide to attack the domestic milk cow and she starts to buck wildly....even though he almost never does and the bucking milk cow jerks her rein strap right out of his right hand. Generally the infant doesn't stand a chance because when the hunter herder microlithic abstract artist shows the saber-toothed cat attacking and clinging on to the top of the bucking milk cow's back, it usually bites off the infant's head before dad can even twitch. This should give you a pretty good idea of how these repetitive themes or folklore tales usually go…….

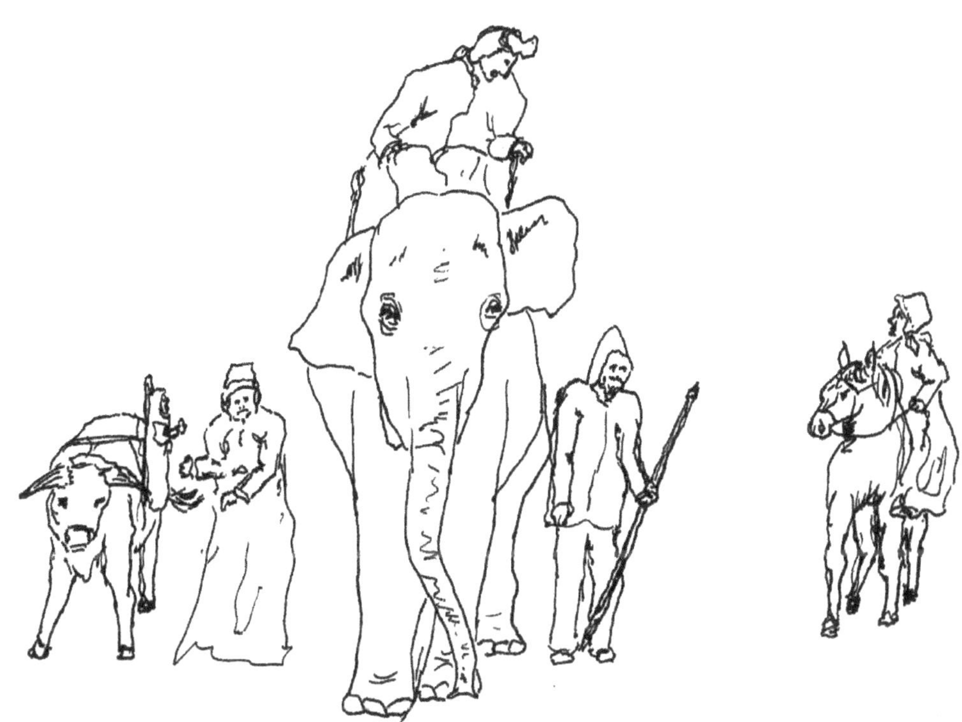

7. The lead family as they trekked in the long
Mammoth People mammoth caravan to…'here'.

Chapter Six

Most Common Folklore Tales

Now I'm going to share with you the most common Mammoth People hunter herder microlithic abstract artist's repetitive themes which are their most common folklore tales. In order to be considered repetitive, I had to have interpreted many pieces with the exact same theme. Then when you get slight variations of that repetitive theme, that variation became part of the complete folklore tale which is how I eventually got the whole story. When I no longer came across a variation, after interpreting dozens of the same repetitive theme I knew that there would be very little to find out by continuing to interpret pieces with that repetitive theme and I would concentrate on the pieces that had any other repetitive theme that I hadn't interpreted very often in hopes of learning more about it. That is unless the piece with the most common repetitive theme had a fantastic combined optical and cognitive illusion close-up image or microlithic cognitive illusion reflection image on it and I knew that it would be a great piece to use to aid in educating the world about the existence of the Caucasian Mammoth People.

These common repetitive themes will help you understand a great deal about the Mammoth Peoples Ice Age lives and the hardships that they endured when they or their ancestors made the long trek to 'here' from their beloved mountainous and volcanic homeland. I'm absolutely convinced that many of these repetitive themes and the majority of the abstract artworks were created in an effort to not only teach the Mammoth People children about the trials and tribulations that their ancestors went through on their epic journey to 'here', but also how to stay safe during the Pleistocene. Many of the teaching themes were found on top of a hill at the '2a' site which is where I'm convinced they had a school. The level of complexity of a piece would have determined the age of the child that would have been studying it and learning to read the Stone Age abstract art figurative language with all of its optical and cognitive illusions along with the etched and rubbed out imagery. Any young student that failed to learn how to read the Stone Age microlithic abstract art figurative language probably failed to survive as well.

Here are the repetitive themes listed more or less in the order that I discovered them, not in the order of which ones are the most common or that are the most popular folklore tales. I saved the two 'most' popular ones towards the end. I have to list all of them because after all, they are the results of my extensive research, so the chapter does get lengthy. Feel free to take breaks when it becomes a little too much....

The Mammoth People mammoth caravan is attacked by two or three marauding saber-toothed cats. There are many versions of this theme and they include all of these scenarios which usually occurred on the potsherd abstract art because one particular pattern that's on the outside side of the potsherds reminded the hunter herder of the hide of a saber-toothed cat....or perhaps the Mammoth People made the pattern that was on the outside side of the potsherd to imitate the hide of the saber-toothed cat…….. They attack from the rear. Two of them climb up the rear end of the running mammoth and work their way towards the mammoth's head that has its ears splayed out on either side of it. The first one jumps down over its head so that it can slice off the end of the mammoth's trunk but since the lead hunter herders head is right there it opts to bite off his head instead. The second saber-toothed cat works excitedly to slice off the mammoth's splayed ears which drop to the ground and end up getting chewed on by rats somewhere back along the chase route. (Have I mentioned that the Mammoth People detested rats?) The third cat runs alongside the mammoths head and tries to jump up and claw at her eyes so that the running mammoth would unintentionally lower her trunk that's raised high in front of her, enough for one of the other saber-toothed cats to grab the mammoth's trunk and slice it off, which was what their long saber fangs were designed to do. (Now we know why still to this day elephants raise their trunks and tails as high as possible when they run from lions.) There's no question in my mind that the Mammoth People also used potsherds that had smooth impressions with crazed lines that looked like wrinkles on the outside sides of them, to imitate mammoth hide.

The second scenario is when one of the saber-toothed cats attacks the back of the domestic milk cow that's usually walking abreast to the right side of the lead mammoth with the infant that's strapped to a backboard slung over her left shoulder. The domestic milk cow and the lead mammoth are always walking abreast of each other because the mammoth's 'all seeing' right eye can see the domestic milk cow's left eye and vice versa. The lead hunter herder's infant is strapped to a backboard and slung over the left shoulder of the domestic milk cow so that he's close to his dad who's walking just ahead of and to the left of the lead mammoth's trunk. Dad and his infant can see each other which give comfort to both of them. In this position dad is close enough to protect his infant, but in most cases that I've seen on the abstract artworks, the infant doesn't stand a chance because the big cats come up from the rear so fast that they jump on the back of the domestic milk cow that then starts 'bucking' wildly and the saber-toothed cat bites off the infants head before dad can do anything. Can you imagine trying to catch a 'bucking' ox or milk cow that has a saber-toothed cat sticking its claws in his or her back and the infant flopping on its left shoulder? I've also seen lions substituted for saber-toothed cats in this repetitive theme. Sometimes they're a male lion and his lioness mate, other times it's a pair of rogue male lions.

The third scenario is when the lead mammoth is pulling the sled that's loaded with grandma and her pregnant ewe and all the little lambs that are too small to walk with the caravan. Grandma sees the marauding saber-toothed cats that are usually coming up fast from the rear. She yells at her son, the lead hunter herder, to RUN. She's very concerned because she's first in line when the saber-toothed cats catch up with them and spring up over the back wall of the sled.

The last scenario is when one of the saber-toothed cats attacks the black faced ram that's usually walking to the left of the lead hunter herder which is also to the left of the mammoth's 'all seeing' left eye. The ram is sometimes featured carrying opposing pottery jars over his shoulders which were probably positioned that way for a quick drink of water as they trekked.

Another common repetitive theme involves the hunter herder taking his inexperienced young lad son hunting. They get in to all kinds of predicaments. In one scenario they go hunting sea lion pups for their soft white pelts because they're the easiest thing for the young lad to kill by clubbing which was when he would bash his wooden club over the innocent looking little sea lion pups head that had big dark 'pleading' eyes.

There are times when the hunter herder and his young lad son become the prey instead of the predators. This is when a saber-toothed cat that's also hunting sea lions decides that they would make a better meal for its cubs. The most common sea lion pup hunting theme involves dad warding off the angry mother sea lion while his inexperienced young lad son tries to club his first helpless sea lion pup. What happens is that the helpless sea lion pup lunges at the unsuspecting inexperienced young lad causing him to recoil backwards temporarily reversing the predator prey rolls. This repetitive theme teaches the youngsters that they can never let their guard down even if they think it's going to be super easy. They also find out that clubbing a baby sea lion pup on the head is 'messier' then they expected when its blood splatters on their faces and hood covered heads.

Another example of when the hunter herder takes his inexperienced young lad son hunting is when they go goose hunting in their camouflaged white kayak wearing white sea lion pup pelt parkas and leggings and even having their faces covered with only a slit for their eyes. The dad is sitting in one end of the kayak and his son is standing up on the other end holding the spear that he's going to launch at a preoccupied Canada goose that's preening its tail feathers. The hunting party looks like a floating piece of snow covered ice and they drift into range at which point the boy launches his spear that pierces the goose's neck. To the proud father this hunt turned his son into a fearless experienced stalking predator hunter because the piece also has the scene of a saber-toothed cat's head engulfing the son's head as if he were being attacked from behind by the saber-toothed cat, when in fact it represented how the proud dad saw his predator son as the fearless stalking saber-toothed cat that he's proudly wearing like a hat and cape. I later realized that the preening goose was really a vain gander that wasn't paying attention to possible predators, only to how he appeared to the female geese. There's always a lesson in the themes that make the waist high young lads and young maidens...aware.

Another common scenario is of the hunter herder and his inexperienced son hiding in the underbrush or behind a tree while they watch three to as many as five lionesses attack the 'Loving Giraffe Family'. The lionesses kill and eat all three of the giraffes. Occasionally the lionesses see the 'not so well hidden' hunter herder and his inexperienced son and they opt to veer off from chasing the giraffe to chasing them. They end up eating the hunter herder and his inexperienced son which must teach the Mammoth People children to stay extremely well hidden….or else.

This next common repetitive theme is of when the young maiden is sitting in the meadow on a stump or rock with her kitty that she always has with her. She's tending her domestic sheep and cattle while she sings sweet Ice Age lullabies or folksongs to her fat kitty that's sitting on her lap. The nearby predators think that her sweet voice is that of a wounded prey animal and they act accordingly, usually attacking from behind and biting down over the top of her bonnet covered head. The predators that attack her range from the saber-toothed cat to the male lion and his lioness mate accomplice, and then there's the big grizzly bear or the pair of dire wolves that cooperate to bring down their helpless prey. Sometimes the young maiden's black Scottish terrier is with her too and the hunter herder microlithic abstract artist makes it clear that while the selfish fat kitty who's always with her, bolts off of his young maiden's lap while she's being attacked and heads for home to save his own fat ass, the Scottie stays to fight whichever predator that's attacking her, to the death to defend his young maiden. You know it's so because you'll see his dead body lying alongside his young maiden or what's left of the young maiden, on her funeral peer which recognizes his importance as a cherished Mammoth People family member.

This repetitive theme is of loving grandma shepherdess who's sitting in the meadow tending the sheep and cattle much like the young maiden theme only she's holding her toddler grandchild whom she's babysitting. The grandchild is usually crying which sounds like a wounded prey animal again and naturally the same aforementioned predators end up attacking the top of unsuspecting kind and loving grandma shepherdess's bonnet covered head from the rear and eating her and her crying toddler grandchild. Sometimes the fat kitty is with grandma and sometimes the black Scottish terrier.

The whole point of the meadow themes was to teach the Mammoth People toddler and older children that any type of noise that they make, whether it's crying, singing or whistling, will attract those big hungry predators. The thought of having your head inside the mouth of a snarling saber-toothed cat, lion, bear or dire wolf should scare you enough to keep your own mouth shut when out in the meadow.

Cremations are another very common theme. I've seen just

about everybody's remains being cremated. And I've learned that the biggest and most extravagant funeral pyres showed the importance of the individual that was being cremated. I have interpreted pieces that show the cremations of infants, mothers, fathers, sons, daughters, grandma, grandpa and even the little black Scottie that was so valuable to the Mammoth People that even he was cremated with the loved one that he died trying to protect. The most moving cremation themes are the ones of young wives or the infant son or daughter or both a wife and son or daughter. The son was obviously incredibly important to the hunter herder artist and you realize this because of the incredible amount of time and effort put into these moving grieving abstract artworks.

This next theme probably should have been mentioned as one of the more common ones because it was just so important to the hunter herder microlithic abstract artisan. That was the theme of reproduction and mating. You'll see anything from the hunter herder's domestic cattle or sheep mating to their domestic mammoth mating. One of the common images that you come across is the domestic bovine or cattle bull in his mating or 'riding' position with wings on his shoulders. The hunter herder artist gives him wings because it just doesn't seem that his rear legs are long enough to get the job done. His hopping rear legs need a little help so that he can get a little more height and finish the job, so the hunter herder microlithic abstract artist gives him wings. It was incredibly important for the cattle, sheep and mammoth to mate successfully. Not only was it important for their domesticated animals to mate successfully it was equally important for the humans. I have several microlithic abstract artworks that represent human procreation. You know when you're seeing them because the young woman that's featured on it looks like her long hair is blowing back behind her and her mouth is opened as if she were singing. She'll look like one of the singing sirens of Greek mythology when in reality she's not upright, she's actually lying on her back with her hair hanging down, and her mouth is wide opened in ecstasy because she appears to be having an orgasm during intercourse and you are viewing the erotic features of her head and face through the eyes of her mate. There's usually quite a few other 'scenes' on the abstract artwork to help depict the mating theme. This is not one that would have been taught the children but rather one that the oversexed young male hunter herder would have made because all he could think about was getting a mate. And he had lots of long boring hours to contemplate mating while he was sitting atop his mammoth herding the cattle, sheep and mammoth which were constantly reminding him of mating. I think that a lot of tied up sexual tension went into making some of the human 'mating stones', as I refer to them.

Another frequent mating theme is that of the male lion and the lioness. He's usually on top of her as she lies with her belly on the ground. His mouth is wide open and her tail is jerking, or twitching from side to side. Her twitching tail is seen when the hunter herder microlithic abstract artist creates multiple images of it in advancing stages which is one of the hunter herder artist microlithic abstract art rules; you can show motion by creating multiple images or a proto-cinema scene. In many cases the mating lions are being watched by a 'peeping tom' young lad hunter herder. The teenage young lad is usually watching them from under a tree that unbeknownst to him has another lioness up in it that's watching him. He usually gets eaten by the male lion and his whole pride after he finishes mating and I think that even though the mating lions are featured in that theme, it actually was used as a teaching tool to teach the Mammoth People children not to stick their big noses where they don't belong. It's about being 'nosy' because the hunter herder microlithic abstract artist shows an optical illusion close-up image of the young lad hunter herder with a big nose. The nosey teenage young lad hunter herder got caught up in the 'sexual' moment and let his guard down long enough to become the mating lion's after-sex snack.

The theme of the dire wolves attacking the sheep is a common theme where the hunter herder microlithic abstract artist always shows the 'submissive ewe' being attacked and bitten on the nape of her neck. The image of the ewe simply submitting is what enlightened me later when I saw the submissive ewe with wings like an angel's wings and that's when I figured out why she was always shown on the death pieces.....she was the 'flying submissive ewe spirit' that glided down from the heavens to suck up the dying or being killed Mammoth People or their domestic animal's, last exhaled breath or 'spirit' and take it back up into the heavens to be with their deceased ancestors. Once I figured that out it always held true and was the for sure way of knowing if someone lived or died in one of the folklore tales.

The regular submissive ewe theme was mostly seen on the long prismatic knife thumb scrapers, or end scrapers which goes to show that if I hadn't moved on to the different sized pieces of flint and heat treated stone utilitarian tools and the other mediums such as potsherds, bone and the grains of sand and gravel that the Mammoth People used for their microlithic abstract art, I wouldn't have gotten as much of the bigger picture that I have to this point in my research. I'd have just found more repetition. It seems that certain utilitarian tools were fashioned to represent certain animals or themes. This explains why I found the birds first. They were on the smallest flake knife debitage which also have the Mammoth People's heads and faces on them, and that's why it took me so long to actually 'find' the Mammoth People because I was only looking for the birds.

The whole prismatic knife thumb scrapers were the forelegs of the attacking predators. They looked just like an attacking dire wolf, saber tooth-cat or lions swiping foreleg and they were the second optical illusion close-up abstract artwork 'form' that I figured out leading to all the other subsequent art form discoveries. The optical illusion close-up image abstract art 'form' that I figured out first though was of the flying birds. The first microlithic abstract artwork that I figured out was the small polished flint irregular shaped stone that had the mating graylag geese on it. It was what I learned about its abstractness that enabled me to expand my 'mind's eye' and eventually figure out the rest of the Mammoth People's microlithic abstract art figurative language.

What if I would have never examined the pottery shards because of what I knew from studying the oldest pottery on the internet? The experts claimed that the oldest pottery in the world wasn't much older than eight thousand years and that was in Japan. I don't know who came up with the theory that humans hadn't acquired that knowledge prior to eight thousand years before present but that's what the consensus believed at the time. Well…the Mammoth People's potsherds can be verified to be theirs simply because of the abstract art themes that are on them and those themes involve Ice Age animals that disappeared thirteen thousand years ago. Consequently, some of the most intriguing discoveries that I've made were made by deciphering the potsherd abstract art figurative language which includes the shaping of the microlithic pieces of sand aggregate that are imbedded in the edges of them, as intricate characters in the scenes that depict the theme. This is why I'm convinced nobody else ever figured anything out. They've been brainwashed by simply attending school. Doors were closed early on that would normally have led to rational thought. The only reason that I started to examine the potsherds more closely was because practically all of the other heat treated flint and the heat treated stone artifacts that were associated with it was Mammoth People abstract art and this would lead one to believe that the potsherds and bone just had to be theirs too. I just couldn't imagine a later culture leaving this much pottery shard debris but nothing else.

Furthermore, I can verify that many of the different arrow and spear point bases were all made by the Mammoth People hunter herders to kill different prey by simply identifying the Mammoth People microlithic abstract art that's on them. They even made large bone harpoon type spear tips for hunting humpback whales that were totally different from the stubby heat treated flint stone spear points that had long girthy shafts that they used to defend themselves from saber-toothed cats and lions. And, many of those harpoon type spear points were made out of mammoth bone...or perhaps whale bone...DNA testing can someday verify that. They had to be made from an animal that large simply because of the circumference of the bone that was needed to create such a large harpoon type point without using the porous marrow or center part of the bone. As usual, I'm drifting off topic. Here are some more repetitive themes...

The theme of when the Mammoth People hunter herder takes his inexperienced son out in their kayak to hunt humpback whales or possibly their calves. Dad can usually be seen holding up his long spear or harpoon. What usually transpires is the male humpback whale breaches up over the kayak and smashes it to smithereens with his whole body. Sometimes he smashes the kayak with his huge fluked tail. In some interpretations both dad and his inexperienced son perish, but in others just the inexperienced lad makes it back to shore along with pieces of the kayak.

The theme of the domesticated cattle's bull charging the bear that's trying to snatch one of his calves is one of the few predator prey themes where the bull appears to get the upper hand, or horn.

The folklore tale of the bull riding rodeo that takes place during the fall festival. This theme is centered on a teenage bull rider whose obviously thrown almost immediately after his bucking bull ride begins. We get to see the proud bull standing in the background while the teenager bends over to dust himself off and pick up his boots and cap that are lying nearby because he was figuratively violently tossed out of them. As he bends over to pick up his cap and boots, we can see the proud bull standing on the other side of him superimposed below the spectator filled grandstand. Amongst the spectators we see the beautiful fair young maiden that the young bull rider was trying too hard to impress but ultimately disappoint. No one was more disappointed in his performance though than his disgusted grandpa who was getting up to leave.

Mammoth standing abreast of each other in a herd with their heads outward to protect the baby mammoth calf or calves from the saber-toothed cats or lions is another common theme.

A pair of dire wolves attacks the fair young maiden or grandma shepherdess who is sitting in the meadow tending their sheep. This is one of my favorite predator prey folklore tales because of the clever way that the hunter herder microlithic abstract artist conveys how the pair of dire wolves work together or cooperate to bring down their prey and make the kill. The 'she' dire wolf always runs from behind the unsuspecting prey victim and barely brushes against her to knock her off guard and off balance while her mate then comes from behind on the other side of the disoriented grandma shepherdess or fair young maiden prey and goes for their exposed throats.

Grandma is supposed to be babysitting her rambunctious toddler grandson when she gets distracted, usually they fall asleep together and take an afternoon nap in the meadow with the sheep, usually by a glacial ice meltwater stream that's rushing like rapids and roaring like a male lion. The rambunctious toddler awakens and is attracted to the bank of the roaring stream. The site of the rushing water causes him to lose his balance he falls in and is seen by his grandma after awakening from his screams, bobbing up and down as he struggles to keep his chin above the frothy choppy water. Spry grandma springs into action and is shown running along the bank and then eventually recovering his drowned body on a sand or gravel bar. The moral of this folklore tale is for youngsters to stay away from the predator glacial ice meltwater 'roaring lion' stream, and for grandmas to not nap when they're babysitting. Sometimes the youngster strays away from the trekker's campsite while the women prepare the evening meal.

The repetitive theme of when the Mammoth People and or their domestic animals fall through the predator ice. I've seen many of the Mammoth People mammoth caravan family members fall through the predator ice and drown at some point throughout all of the interpretations. One of the most common is of the waist high young maiden or young lad falling through a snow covered or iced over sea lion breathe hole when mom should have been holding on to their hands and not gossiping with grandma as they trekked across the predator ice and eventually to 'here'. Many times there's the theme of mom going down and getting smashed between the right side of the mammoth and the left side of the domestic milk cow that she's walking between because that's where her and her infant that's strapped to a backboard and slung over the left shoulder of the domestic milk cow are supposed to be the safest from surprise attacking predators like saber-toothed cats and lions.

Unfortunately, when they get on thin ice the combined weight of the mammoth and the domestic milk cow collapse the ice and like a big trap door it swallows mom, the mammoth, the milk cow and the infant. Mom gets crushed between them on the way down and then the ice closes up behind them after they fall through it, like a big trap door. In almost every 'falling through the predator ice' theme the prey victim is often shown floating supine with their faces pressed up against the bottom or the underside of the ice with their mouths wide opened gulping for air and sometimes trying to suck air bubbles on the bottom of the ice while they claw frantically to find the hole that they fell through. The other family members that include other siblings or the milk cow, ram or kitty are usually the ones peering intently down through the ice to see the predator ice's prey victim's sad desperate images as they drown.

The most gripping predator ice folklore tale is of when the fair young maiden falls through the predator ice along with her horse that she's riding. The predator ice seems to swallow them up like a trap door and the struggling fair young maiden ends up drifting along below the predator ice face up clawing for air and the hole that she fell through while her helpless lead hunter herder dad is down on all fours on the ice with his hood covered head down to it and his wide open disbelieving eyes peering through the ice at his supine drowning fair young maiden daughter's horrified face that's pressed up against the underside of the predator ice while hysterical mom stands bent over behind dad helplessly looking down too. They're both helpless and unable to do a thing about their beautiful fair young maiden daughter's demise except to watch her drown and then slowly sink into the dark icy cold abyss.

One distinctive version of this theme takes place after grandma dismounts from the mammoth that she's riding atop on her special armchair from where she was conversing with her fair young maiden granddaughter while they were trekking abreast of each other before the fair young maiden's horse broke through the predator ice. This is the most common version of the predator ice folklore tales and in it grandma spryly dismounts from the nervous lead mammoth, runs and plops down on her belly on the edge of the hole in the predator ice and extends her shepherds crook or cane out towards her fair young maiden granddaughter who's struggling to keep her chin above the icy cold water that's being churned up into a froth by her thrashing horses flailing forelegs and hooves. Dad kneels down behind grandma and holds down on the backs of her legs so that she can extend as much of her upper body out over the edge of the hole in the predator ice as possible. Mom frantically directs the nervous lead mammoth to come and kneel down on the edge of the ice next to grandma and dad, and extend her long tusks out over the hole so grandma can hang on to one of them with her free hand while she uses the other to extend her long shepherds crook as far out as possible towards the struggling fair young maiden. While she's extending her shepherds crook towards her fair young maiden granddaughter, she also has to shove back the thrashing horse's head and try to keep his flailing front feet's hooves from not only kicking her in the face but also from kicking the fair young maiden in the head and knocking her unconscious. The thrashing horse thinks that his lead family is trying to rescue him first.

Sometimes the cooperation between the lead family that includes the nervous lead mammoth saves the fair young maiden and her horse and this teaches a valuable lesson to the Mammoth People children about cooperation. Other times the lack of cooperation seems to be the driven home point of the storyline when they don't manage to save the fair young maiden. Sometimes they can't save her but the mammoth still manages to pull the struggling horse out by the neck with her long strong trunk and save him because after all, he is a family member too. You always know when they don't save the fair young maiden though because the flying submissive ewe spirit will be close at hand. She's seen either waiting patiently on the ice in a submissive posture or she's seen actually gliding down and diving through the hole in the predator ice right past grandma's head to suck up the drowning fair young maiden's last exhaled breath which is her spirit that the submissive ewe spirit carries into the heavens to be with the Mammoth Peoples deceased loved ones.

The 'flying submissive ewe spirit' is as entrenched in the Mammoth Peoples psyche as the cross or crucifix is to modern day Christians. She delivers or blows out of her mouth the marriage or unity blessing and the newborn baby blessing while she retrieves or sucks up the dying Mammoth Peoples spirits which are their last exhaled breaths and takes them back into the heavens to be with their deceased ancestors.

The rare theme of the windblown prairie grass fire that shows the Pleistocene animals and Mammoth People running for their lives out ahead of it in a line. One interpretation showed giraffes running abreast with the horses and mammoth and was being seen by a flying grouse that was also flying abreast of them and as high as the giraffe's heads.

Another one showed mom and dad trying to wet down the thatched gabled roof of their cottage while their fair young maiden daughter took her two rambunctious younger brothers, the milk cows, the mammoth and the horse to stand in the river while she called for her fat kitty. It turned out that the predator windblown prairie grass fire is the only predator that I've ever seen be able to kill the fat kitty. He always gets away when other predators attack the fair young maiden or grandma out in the meadow because he bails and runs for home while the ferocious Scottish terrier dog stays to fight and defend them to the death. In this particular theme though I found out that the fat kitty always runs for the cottage and its safety but he couldn't get in this time because mom and dad were trying to put out fires on the roof with river water that was being bucketed from the river by mom. Dad was throwing it on the burning roof so the frightened kitty opted to find safety in the barn instead which is where the fire got him along with one of the favorite milk cows.

The last folklore tale reminded me of the herd stead yard theme. This theme shows different activities that take place on the herd stead yard such as shearing sheep or working the sheep and milking cows. There was one awesome piece in particular that showed grandma milking one of the cows out in the meadow and then walking back to the gabled thatch roofed cottage where she gave the milk to her crying infant grandson that she was babysitting...but while she was gone, a rat had climbed into the baby's crib and was starting to nibble on his ears. The barking Scottie that was with grandma out in the meadow alerted her to the crying infant that she left unattended.

One of the most fascinating repetitive themes which I'm confident was the basis of many folklore tales, featured birth. I've interpreted many birth themes that show the hunter herder assisting in sheep and mammoth birth. After he helps 'pull' or deliver the newborn he always is shown getting it to nurse which as you can imagine was extremely difficult when you consider holding up a baby mammoth with one arm and trying to get its mouth on one of the mother mammoth's teats with his other hand and doing it right behind one of her huge forelegs that could easily kick you away from her. In some birth themes mom is usually shown carting off the newborn lamb to the cottage to be dried off by the warm hearth of the fireplace with one of her inquisitive waist high children following her and asking all kinds of birth questions. One interpretation has mom assisting a cow that was having a calf while her fair young milk maiden daughter stood by the cow's head and the inquisitive waist high young maiden daughter stood behind mom asking relentless birth questions. The best birth themes and the rarest ones are of human birth. One in particular was created on a piece that was the color and shape of the placenta which obviously had a very important meaning. I found it very interesting to learn that the Mammoth People herdswoman delivered their babies bent over on all fours just like all of their domesticate animals did. She was always assisted by her mother or a midwife that catches the baby's supine head. The baby was always born face up and after he or she is born the mother turns around and sits on the bed to deliver the placenta or afterbirth which must have held some great importance to the Mammoth People.

I saved this repetitive theme or folktale for now on purpose because I felt that if I mentioned it earlier you would think I've gone off the deep end and am now writing pure fiction...that is if any or all of the aforementioned repetitive themes haven't already made you think that. The fact that you are still reading this far into this book implies that you must think that there's some semblance of believability to it without having actually seen the microlithic abstract artworks that I've interpreted the microlithic abstract art figurative language on....or you're just being entertained in an outlandish sort of way. Either way, the Mammoth People's folklore tales will be 'implanted' in your 'mind's eye' which is ultimately what I set out to do...

One of the most important themes that I've repeatedly come across has an incredible amount of anthropological significance when it comes to who the earliest human occupants of this North American continent were. For me, it explains just about everything especially if we find that the Mammoth People's occupancy was basically 'here' in the center of the North American continent where I've conducted my research on them. I believe that from here all the way to the east and the west coasts was always occupied by the Palomino Pony People. I'm now convinced that this location from where I wright this book in the center of the North American continent, is the western fringe area of their occupancy. Directly east of here was the retreating Laurentide Ice Sheet or glacier that dipped all the way to what is now southern Iowa. I have a two foot wide red granite glacial erratic 'bust' (minus the shoulders) that has the left side view of the gruff chiefs head on it that helps verify this assumption because it had to have been used by the Mammoth People as a warning stone. It was placed on my Grandpa Hruska's farmland that is just a couple of miles southeast of where I live and write this book, and is where I still farm today. The large red granite glacial erratic had to have been on the top of one of the loess clay hills above the flowing springs because that would have been a great place to get running spring water that was enriched with iron. I can picture it as an east to west travel route. It was a warning stone for any Mammoth People who lived here alerting them to the dangers of entering the Palomino Pony People occupied territories that were further to the east between here and the retreating glacier.

These no doubt, were the people referred to by archeologist as the Clovis culture but to me they are the Palomino Pony People because their young warrior braves ride 'running like the wind' or galloping palomino horses. Sometimes the braves have shaved head tops with long black hair coming off the sides of their heads and being blown back because their horses are galloping so fast. Sometimes their long black hair is in a ponytail and sometimes it's just loose and blowing back just like the mane of the galloping horse that always has his head and neck portrayed as if it's reaching for the finish line in a race. Its nostrils are flared, its eyes are wide opened and there are even images of a bridle and reins coming from its mouth along with frothy slobber. The reddish skinned warrior braves mouth is portrayed wide open with his tongue in the middle of it which looks like its warbling as if he were whooping and hollering as he and his galloping horse run circles around the Mammoth People mammoth caravan that they raid. The lead hunter herder and his awestruck son watch from in front of the nervous lead mammoth while a warrior brave and his 'running like the wind' or galloping palomino horse are seen chasing the fair young maiden who's running screaming for her life towards her dad with her bonnet flying back behind her blond head that usually shows blond pigtails.

When the caravan is brought to a halt by the lead hunter herder or 'dad', the gruff chief, who always has a big hooked nose and a gruff looking face, comes up to talk to the lead hunter herder face to face. They have a 'powwow' right there in front of the nervous lead mammoth's trunk, which usually ends up fishing over the lead hunter herder's shoulders to touch his bearded face for reassurance because she's just as nervous as the other female trekkers. Neither dad nor the gruff chief has anything to say because their mouths remain closed since they don't understand each other's spoken language. If the gruff chief isn't seen wearing a single eagle feather on his head, he'll be wearing an eagle feather headdress with its long trains running down either side of him.

This reminds me to mention that the warrior braves are usually shown with a single eagle feather tied to the hair on the side of their heads....or they may also be shown wearing an eagle feather headdress like the one that the gruff chief is wearing. The lead hunter herder and the gruff chief are face to face and waiting to have their speechless powwow and are usually shown as 'opposing heads' with nothing to say to each other or nothing in common. Many times there is no powwow and you see the gruff chief watching over the massacre from a high spot. Every one of the Mammoth People caravan members gets speared....albeit that is a rare variation of the folklore tale.

The repetitive theme of the 'powwow' represents the friction between the two cultures. I get the distinct impression after interpreting so many of the microlithic abstract artworks, that the Mammoth People boldly trekked into the occupied territories of the Palomino Pony People in their long mammoth caravan and that eventually after they had settled here for a while, they were at all-out war. I have one microlithic abstract artwork that shows where a

Palomino Pony People warrior brave was riding around a disbelieving Mammoth People hunter herder who was observing the spear that was thrown and that stuck in the spine of one of his invaluable white ewes while its lamb looked on.

Then I have an absolutely priceless flint war club microlithic abstract artwork that shows the Mammoth People hunter herders getting slaughtered by the Palomino Pony People warrior braves that were riding their palomino horses and were clearly the ones that were attacking. You can easily tell who's who on this piece because the Mammoth People hunter herder wore a hat that looked like a summertime vintage sailor style hat that was high in the front with a short visor on it and that sloped back to a point between his shoulders. He had flesh colored skin while the warrior braves had long black hair. The gist of that piece was that in that bloody hand to hand exchange, every Palomino Pony People warrior brave was killing at least two Mammoth People hunter herders with their swinging war clubs while the Mammoth People hunter herders were fighting with hand held spears. The warrior braves war club was smashing one of the Caucasian Mammoth People hunter herders in the mouth as he rode by on his galloping horse and the fantastic microlithic abstract artwork masterpiece was showing that there were two warrior braves for each hunter herder.

The implications of this one abstract artwork alone are mind blowing because it would verify what I always suspected from the beginning when I started to interpret the Mammoth People hunter herder microlithic abstract artworks. That is that it seemed to me that such valuable personalized artworks would never have been lost especially right on the Mammoth People hunter herder's herd steads. I always figured that if an asteroid didn't wipe them out right where they slept then something else did and that something else could have easily been the Palomino Pony People warrior braves who raided their herd steads. They could have stormed in on each individual herd stead one by one and easily eradicated the Caucasian Mammoth People family that lived there. By centering their culture on the horse the Palomino Pony People one-upped the Mammoth People because of the element of speed. And just like modern day technologies, speed wins every time. The mammoth may have had the strength of ten horses but a ten horse power slow machine can't compete when it comes to getting from point 'a' to point 'b' in the shortest amount of time in the most efficient manner. It also entertains the notion that the Palomino Pony People could have killed every mammoth that they saw just to prevent the spread of the Caucasian Mammoth People. This would have started a collapse in the Pleistocene mega mammal fauna ecosystem because of the symbiotic predator prey relationship between the mammoth and the saber-toothed cats and lions. Then when you throw in the Younger Dryas, but more probable, the Older Dryas (because there were still lions and giraffes around) and a mini Ice Age you can see how the Palomino Pony People that were already down in the southwestern part of the North American continent, would have had the advantage to survive and move back in and occupy the rest of the North American continent perhaps a thousand years later.

There are many other themes that I've come across but they weren't necessarily repetitive which means that they're more like 'doodling' by the hunter herder who was simply passing time as he herded his domestic mammoth, cattle, sheep, and even giraffes or when he was waiting patiently for prey when he was hunting. Perhaps he simply wanted to bring out something that he saw in the stone or potsherd and it reminded him of an incident in his everyday life so he created a storyline around it. Here are a few of them……

…..The theme of the predator white lightning bolt hitting the top of the mammoth's domed head top. Sometimes he has a passenger atop his back. This can be a hunter herder but most likely it will be grandma. They'll be trekking along in their Mammoth People mammoth caravan in a thunderstorm when the predator white lightning bolt strikes. I'm convinced that this earlier theme that I figured out was simply the repetitive 'volcanic mass exodus' theme before I knew it existed and that the lightning was coming from the ash cloud that was pursuing the fleeing trekkers.

….The fair young maiden or a herdswoman milking the cow.

….The lambs nursing the ewe.

….Snakes attacking ducklings.

….The vulture flying over the kill site waiting to take his turn while the lioness lounges after she had her fill.

….The huge python size snake striking at the mammoth's neck when the mammoth stepped on it in the marsh.

….The waist high young lad peeking over the window sill of the gabled thatched roof sod walled cottage to see mom and dad coming home in the oxen pulled sled.

….The glassless window openings of the cottage are used in other themes. Someone looking out the window usually signifies that somebody hasn't come home and it's getting late which usually doesn't bode well for that somebody. In one potsherd abstract artwork the young maiden was running for the cottage while being chased by a saber-toothed cat...sometimes it's a grizzly bear. Mom was looking out one of the windows of the cottage and a kitty was looking out the other one. She never made it and mom saw the whole tragic attack event.

….One touching potsherd theme was about a young family's toddler son falling down the herd stead's well and drowning. The grieving father strips down to his underwear and crawls down what looks like tied together sheets with knots. He pulls the drowned toddler out with the sheets that are tied to his bundled up body.

….One flint theme had a mammoth drinking with his trunk through a hole in the ice.

….Then there's the beaver themes where the hunter herder artist uses the grey nodular flint to produce the effects of the rings of a tree that the beaver chewed down. Many times you'll see the beaver looking back at you from his den hole in the bank of the river.

….One theme showed a raccoon trapped in the back of a hollow log.

….Then there's the wicked bald eagle themes. Sometimes the eagle is diving to get a goose's goslings or a turkey's chicks. There's one theme of the young maiden in the meadow protecting her lambs from the wicked black bald eagle that was trying to swoop down and snatch one up. He always has the characteristic white head and neck collar. They were gliding black wicked predators to the Mammoth People, not something that they would have made into a national symbol.

….And I can't forget the theme of the hunter herder going out to revenge kill the saber-toothed cat and hang him by his neck in a tall tree. The hunter herder's 'thumbs up' hand that was wrapped around the rope that was pulling the 'hunted down and killed' saber-toothed cat, up over the tree branch, left an unforgettable image in my 'mind's eye'.

…..Another cottage theme piece that I interpreted on 5/2/16 was titled... 'The family had just started eating their porridge when the hungry bear burst through the top half of the Dutch door, uninvited!

Then there's the horrifying folklore tale of when mom herdswoman took her daughters to the mother daughter gathering and over stayed into the twilight hour. That's usually when the hungry dire wolves were coming out to find something to eat...which they did. The pack chased the ox pulled sled that had mom standing in the front of it mushing the running ox as hard as she could while her two horrified daughters clung to the top of the front wall of the sled with the running ox's excrement splashing all over the fronts of them. The folklore tale usually doesn't end well for the exhausted ox that just couldn't pull the sled any faster in the deep snow with a snarling dire wolf hanging from each of his ears, nor does it end well for the occupants of the sled. One of the pieces that I interpreted showed a combined optical and cognitive illusion close-up image of the glove covered hand of eaten mom herdswoman lying on the ground in the position that it had been mushing, with the ox's excrement splattered all over it. The moral of that folklore tale was simply to scare the young maidens...and their mother so that they wouldn't get carried away gossiping at their mother daughter gatherings and lose track of Pleistocene time because their very lives depended on it...

The roaring 'epic deluge' that swept the Mammoth People away while they were trekking to 'here' is a repetitive theme that most cultures seem to have come up with down through the millennia that emphasizes a great flooding event, but this one I believe actually happened and I believe that there's proof that it happened on an immense scale. This epic deluge or great flood was caused by the breach of a glacial ice dam wall that held back a huge lake of glacial ice meltwater. No doubt, that near the end of the last glaciation there would have been numerous flooding events like this but the one featured on the hunter herders microlithic abstract art is one of truly monumental proportions. It was an 'epic deluge'. The proof is on the piece called 2/20/12 'pure abstract art'... 'The roaring male lion and his stalking lioness mate breached the glacial ice dam wall and unleashed an epic deluge on the trekking Mammoth People!' This piece is about a glacial ice dam breaching and releasing an immense amount of water from a glacial lake that's looking more and more like Lake Missoula that was repeatedly dammed by the advancing Cordilleran Ice Sheet. Every time that it breached over the millennia it released epic amounts of water from Lake Missoula that reached back into present day Montana. Over time the epic floods carved out the Channeled Scab Lands of central Washington State which is a basalt plain that had been created by repeated lava flows over millions of years.

I believe that the Mammoth People simply trekked on the Pacific Ocean's frozen over summer sea ice sheet along its southern most edge from their volcanic homeland of Northern Japan or the southern part of the Kamchatka Peninsula of Eastern Russia, all the way to present day Washington State. They didn't want to live in another land of volcanoes once they made landfall so they kept moving east across the Channeled Scab Lands where they happened to get in on the last of the epic floods before the glaciers retreated and quit cutting off the Clark Fork River that went through the Colombia Gorge. When this gorge was blocked by the advancing ice sheet it created Lake Missoula. I'm absolutely convinced that this is the lake featured in the 'epic deluge' repetitive theme because of the shoreline strandlines that could be seen on the inside side of the dammed lake that was on one of the pieces that I interpreted this repetitive theme on. This epic deluge would verify that the Mammoth People hugged the southern shoreline of the sea ice while they crossed the ocean, instead of funneling down the gap between the Cordilleran and Laurentide ice sheets after crossing the Bearing straight. They crossed the Channeled Scablands to the 'drained' lake Missoula and then they simply crossed the Rocky's, went across the gap in the ice sheets and then followed the southern edge of the Laurentide ice sheet to where it dipped down which was about to the edge of northern Nebraska. Further east it dipped down to the southern border of what is now Iowa which is why they would have turned and headed south ending up in what is now Butler County, Nebraska. A Serengeti type environment awaited them with no epic floods, no predator ice and no volcanoes. Basically, no more fire and ice.

When you see images of the swimming mammoth in the repetitive theme or folklore tale of the 'epic deluge', the whole swimming mammoth can be represented by just the image of her flapping ears, her snorkel trunk or her swimming 'kicking' legs and feet that you would see as combined optical and cognitive illusion close-up images that along with grandma who's sitting atop her on her special armchair and steering her with her long cane or shepherd's crook, would have everything else reflecting off of them as microlithic cognitive illusion reflection images. The two of them are usually shown desperately rescuing the rest of the lead family with the help of dad and his strong swimming teenage young lad son and his vivacious fair young maiden daughter. They rescue the elderly first which happens to be grandpa and then they rescue mom and her infant, her toddlers and then the rest of the sibling children. Everyone gets hoisted up on the back of the swimming lead mammoth until she's weighted down in the churning glacial ice meltwater that has chunks of ice floating in it. Even the swimming lead mammoths own struggling baby mammoth gets hoisted up over her rear ends hips, and after everyone is onboard behind grandma's special armchair, the waist high young maiden has a sobbing fit because she can't find her grey kitty so everyone shouts out for him calling.... "Precious!" while they look intently for him from the back of the swimming mammoth.

Lost Precious paddles frantically towards them, periodically raising one of his front paws to try to wave at them and get their attention. They do eventually rescue their last lost family member and he's shown reuniting with his emotional waist high young maiden as she hangs onto the back of grandma's special armchair while the rest of the family is shown jubilantly rejoicing on the back of the swimming lead mammoth that's using her trunk as a snorkel because the weight on her back has submerged her head. And in case you're wondering, grandma steered her to high ground by tapping the sides of her submerged head with her long shepherd's crook...sometimes the high ground had other swept away Mammoth People clinging to it.

I figured out this next repetitive theme because I chose to focus on human or anthropological images. What I found was that most of them are on the heat treated more colorful flint abstract artworks. Once I was on to it I found many of these humanistic themed abstract artworks in succession and it became one of the Mammoth Peoples top two dominant repetitive themes, one that venerated or paid special tribute to the trials and tribulations of their ancestors who made the epic journey to 'here' the very place that I've been conducting this research. This repetitive theme or most told folklore tale is of the 'volcanic mass exodus' and is similar to how modern American's paid special tribute to their pioneering families that trekked across this great North American continent in long wagon trains...only...they weren't the first Caucasian ones to do so albeit the first ones did it in a long 'mammoth' caravan that will be described later. This one however is the repetitive theme of the Mammoth People fleeing their beloved volcanic homeland in a mass exodus when an erupting volcano went ballistic in the middle of the Pleistocene night. The multitudes of miserable weary Mammoth People are shown walking, climbing and descending as they tried to escape the 'roaring' volcanoes broiling ash cloud that's creeping over them like the 'anvil' of a thunderstorm cloud with white lightning bolts flashing in and out of it. The leading edge of the broiling ash cloud is depicted as the extended foreleg and paw of a roaring and attacking male lion that appears to be swiping at or pouncing on its prey. Not only will you see him in scenes of the anvil of the broiling ash cloud that's relentlessly chasing the fleeing Mammoth People, but you'll also see him roaring in a pyroclastic flow that's racing through the valley below the volcano. It's usually in its own separate theme though and it was on one of those pieces that I learned once and for all that the Mammoth People built cottages with gabled thatched roofs with a chimney in the middle of its gabled peak, in their volcanic homeland, wherever it was. I still believe it was on the southern tip of the Kamchatka Peninsula of eastern Russia or the northern part of Japan.

Once I found the 'volcanic mass exodus' repetitive theme or folklore tale I also found multiple other human interaction themes such as the 'spring or summertime' picnic one that shows the young teenage hunter herder and the fair young maiden wandering off down to the riverbank where there were a lot of trees and underbrush cover. There they would proceed to strip down and make out. Unbeknownst to them there would be a sneaky waist high young lad smirking while he watched from up in a tree above them or who was simply smirking while he watched through the underbrush because he was inadvertently alerted to the hidden couple by his bloodhound pup that had found a nesting goose in the same underbrush. He then reports what he saw to grandma and the next thing you see is the lovebirds being chased out of the underbrush in front of the huge picnic crowd by the mortified fair young maiden's irate grandmother who was wielding her shepherd's crook and who was tipped off by one of those nosey ornery waist high young lads and his bloodhound pup. He was most likely the mortified fair young maiden's ornery little brother. These pieces are extremely interesting to say the least and I'm sure the lesson to all of the fair young maidens that it was told to was to never sneak off into the underbrush with a beau if you want to be spared immense embarrassment.

Another common repetitive theme that involves a large gathering of Mammoth People and a pompous boisterous magistrate is one that I call the 'jilted forlorn lover' theme. It shows a pompous boisterous plump but fancily dressed magistrate marrying a couple on a hillside in the springtime. The hunter herder abstract artist focuses on the jilted forlorn lover who's prematurely leaving the wedding ceremony because he knows for certain that he lost the beautiful fair young maiden bride to another who was more handsome than he. He's shown sulking off towards the hitching post where the mammoth and the horses are tied and while he's untying his mare from the hitching post, the giraffe that's feeding on the uppermost succulent leaves of a tree that's on the other side of the hitching post, lowers her head down to sniff the tearful jilted forlorn lovers face. On most of these pieces with this repetitive theme, almost all of the imagery is reflecting off of the combined optical and cognitive illusion and in some cases 'statuesque' close-up image of the curious giraffe's head because it goes from having her snout that has her long tongue reaching upwards towards the most succulent leaves, to where her sniffing snout is pointing down towards the jilted forlorn lovers tearful face and as you rotate the piece through those exact motions, you see both the further away and the closer up overlapping microlithic reflection images and scenes that are reflecting off of it. It's how these 'rotational change-up' microlithic abstract artworks function. Sometimes the jilted forlorn lover can be seen riding his mare off into the purple hues of the Pleistocene sunset...with a broken heart.

The theme that involves the plump pompous boisterous magistrate conducting a wedding ceremony on a hillside isn't always about a jilted forlorn lover though. I interpreted one that was about the extremely sad dad who was losing his extremely happy fair young maiden daughter bride to another. This piece was most definitely created by the extremely sad father who was very close to his fair young maiden daughter and most likely depended on her to do a lot of the chores around the herd stead like milking the cows. It had images of his fair young 'milk' maiden waving goodbye to him over the back of the 'just married' sled that was being pulled by a draft horse.

From all of the repetitive Mammoth People hunter herder microlithic abstract art repetitive folklore tales, especially this 'jilted forlorn lover' one that shows the wedding ceremony and the boisterous pompous plump magistrate holding up his hands over the just married couple and bestowing the 'flying submissive ewe spirits' unity blessing on them, I've come to realize that the Mammoth People were basically loving empathetic folks like modern day Christians long before 'Christ' and his angels that have wings that look exactly like the flying submissive ewe spirit's wings...... the proof is rock solid.....the bride even wears a white dress and white veil and the dashing groom wears black. The Mammoth People microlithic abstract art verifies that the human mind is hardwired to perceive things that are really not there (pareidolia)... like the 'flying submissive ewe spirit' that was as close as you can get to modern humans imagined 'flying angels'. Caucasians have passed that notion down to the present and we are no doubt seeing it still in the angels and the 'lamb of god' images of modern day religions Christianity....

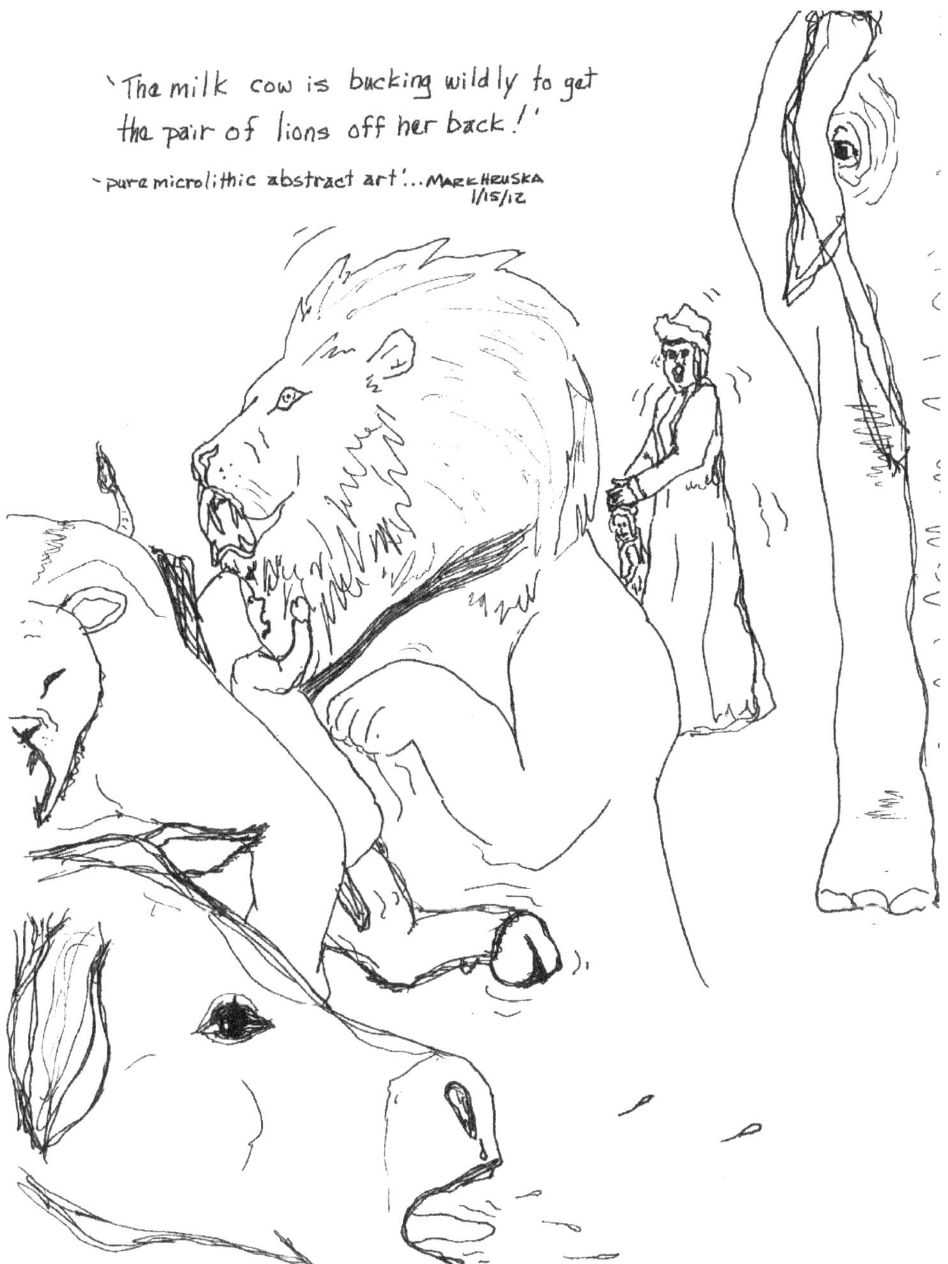

8. Mom and dad had no warning or chance to stop the domestic milk cow
from bucking away from them with the pair of lions on her back.

Chapter Seven

What to Make of Them and Their Art

When I first figured out the Stone Age abstract art figurative language and didn't know that it was the work of the Caucasian Mammoth People, all I was 'seeing' was all of this bird art because I didn't know what else I should be looking for so I kept studying what I knew was real with the hope of one day getting a glimpse of the folks who were creating it. The theme on many of the bird microlithic abstract artworks involved mother birds standing in the nest and protecting or feeding their chicks. One was the theme of a mother duck with her wings hovering over her ducklings while they walked. These were some of the first pieces where I learned about the hunter herder microlithic abstract artist's abstract art techniques. You had to imagine in your 'mind's eye' to be in the ground looking straight up underneath that mother duck and her ducklings and see exactly what they looked like from underneath her feet. Or that you could see through the bottom of a nest and see what it looked like beneath the mother bird that had her feet around the hatching eggs.

This opened up a whole new window of cognition for me that enabled me to decipher the Stone Age microlithic abstract art figurative language because shortly afterward I found 'the supine old woman being burnt on her funeral pyre', by simply looking underneath the flickering flames and rising smoke images to see what she looked like laying there. But she wasn't the first image of the Caucasian Mammoth People that I first saw. The very first time that I got an eye opening glimpse of them was when I saw the microlithic 'head of a pin' sized image of crotchety grandma's head and face as she sat of all places....on top of a 'walking towards you' mammoth and she seemed to be sitting on a special armchair. Not only did I instantaneously find the Caucasian race of folks that had lived here all of those millennia ago, but on the very same piece, I saw that they were living with the mammoth...their domesticated mammoth. Up until I saw crotchety grandma's microlithic face above the 'walking towards you mammoth' where she sat on her special armchair, I had thought that the microlithic abstract art was being created by the red skinned Native American Indian's ancestors. Crotchety grandma's microlithic white face was the first time that I entertained the notion that perhaps the art was being created by a Caucasian culture that had lived here too and that they had been displaced and were searching for a new home that a red skinned culture had already occupied.

First I found the ducks and geese and deciphered the microlithic abstract arts figurative language by understanding how you could envision their whole bodies on 'rotational change-ups' with their long necks wrapped around the front of one of their flapping wings (represented by the whole prismatic knife or oval knife), and then I figured out the different microlithic abstract art 'rules' and art 'forms' which led me to finding other animal's heads like the bovine bull or ox, the ram, the horse, the ewe and the mammoth, and then lions and saber-toothed cats. Only then did I find the gruff chief's eagle feather headdress covered head and gruff looking face that appears much as it always did right up through recent historic times. The last thing that I found was the Caucasian Mammoth People themselves because it's really difficult to find something that you don't know you're looking for. Having so much of the imagery of their heads and faces on the smallest flint flake knives or what you'd consider debitage, didn't help any.

Once I found them though, I devoted all of my time and attention to seeing them because they seemed to be who actually created all of the microlithic abstract artworks with everything else but themselves on it....until I realized that I had been looking at mostly the biggest pieces of spear points, knives and debris when most of the images of them were actually on the smallest flake knives or debitage, the pottery sherds and bone and gravel....yes gravel. I called them 'gravel heads' and I found them after I realized that small white, pink or red pieces of tiny sand aggregate that's embedded in the edges of the potsherds were the heads and faces of the characters of their repetitive themes or folklore tales. In fact, like the bigger 'gravel heads' that are found individually, many of the tiny flake knives 'are' the images of the Mammoth People's heads and faces too... bonnets and all. It's safe to speculate that not a single piece of the Mammoth Peoples flint debitage is discarded waist. Every single piece is microlithic abstract art...even the pieces of gravel. It was like figuring out that they couldn't use a single tool without paying homage and respect to their ancestors for enduring the trials and tribulations on their epic journey to 'here'.

Once this realization set in....it was off to the proverbial races identifying them and their nemesis the Palomino Pony People. But lions were also their nemesis in so many of their folklore tales, like when they wanted to show something attacking them, they perceived it as the roaring male lion's swiping paw. Examples would be when they show the broiling ash cloud that's about to pounce on them when they flee the violently erupting volcano that chased them out of their beloved mountainous homeland, or the roaring epic deluges monstrous wave that looks like it's a swiping male lion's paw that's about to crash down on the unsuspecting trekkers, or the roaring male lion lahar that's sweeping through the valley of their homeland community...often with his lioness mate running by his side.

The process to actually find the Mammoth People was long and arduous and could only have been discovered in the scientific research manner in which I proceeded, starting with the image of the duck's bill that was sticking out of the side of a thumb scraper which progressed to finding a highly worked and polished small piece of grey flint that had no knife edges on it and that I correctly deciphered as being 'mating' graylag geese. That piece alone brought the realization that I was viewing complex abstract art that reminded me of cubism, Picasso and modernist art. The method that was used to figure out and decipher that piece never changed and it gave me the 'rules' to follow from then on including the one that states; once you find microlithic abstract art on one side of the piece, every other side must also have art on it, meaning that it must be in some way part of the whole artwork.

Once I understood that I was dealing with people who are...or...were more intelligent then I was, I could begin to think in that manner as if I were playing an intense chess game with them that they won because for me what before was incomprehensible was now a solid realization that their very existence depended on. And since it was a microlithic abstract art involving folklore tales entwined with their knife scraper eating utensils, I also realized that it was going to be extremely difficult to educate the rest of the world of their existence.

Then when I figured out that optical illusions and cognitive illusions were an intricate part of their microlithic abstract art figurative language the stage was set to discover everything else… Just think of all the stories waiting to be told right now in all the museums and private collections all over the continent and then on across Asia and into Europe where they originated. I feel strongly that they had to have moved across the Balkans and then Russia before ending up at Kamchatka. They brought that Stone Age microlithic abstract art figurative language from the lands of the British Isles, Scotland and Europe and I know it's there to be studied and taken back as far as we can take it. This microlithic abstract art figurative language could have possibly been around for millennia. That's not to say that they didn't have a literal language because I know that they definitely did. The Mammoth People definitely had more astute cognitive and dexterity skills then we do today and I actually have 'opposing head' images of them talking to each other, reminiscing and telling stories. They were in each other's heads thinking the same thoughts….and they were storytellers.

Everything that I identified and gave a name to on the Mammoth People hunter herder microlithic abstract art was given its identity the first time that I saw it. I never changed what I called something after I identified it the first time....like naming the Mammoth People just that after seeing them atop their domesticated mammoth that they rode and that pulled their sleds, or the Palomino Pony People after the golden 'sulfur' or palomino horses that the gruff chief and his crazy warrior braves rode. Even the submissive ewe spirt that was always portrayed with her head down flat on the ground as if she submitted when a predator jumped on her back and bit down on the nape of her neck, was always recognized as a submissive ewe....and then I found out that on some of the pieces she had wings and flew thus becoming the flying submissive ewe spirit. She is the most prominent image in all of the Mammoth Peoples microlithic abstract art because her presence either means that someone is dying and she's swooping down to suck up their last exhaled breath which is their spirit or she's swooping down to deliver or blow out a spirit at birth or during a union of a couple that's getting married or hitched.

Nothing has changed. We've only just stepped out of the Stone Age. If we return we won't survive at the level that our ancestors did because we've forgotten all of the necessary things that it would take to survive without electricity. The planet is going to keep spinning no matter what we do to it. I just can't help myself but to try to imagine in my 'mind's eye' where our culture will be thirteen thousand years into the future. I am convinced that we are never going to get off of this rock and that we had better prepare for the long haul ahead because this is as good as it gets and that's precisely how our ancestors felt when they found this bountiful land that was void of fire and ice.

Everyone thinks that Mesopotamia was the cradle of civilization. I can honestly tell you that there were other civilizations living elsewhere long before Mesopotamia. Can anyone show me another civilization that existed alongside the mammoth and saber-toothed cats? Over thirteen thousand years ago a sophisticated Caucasian civilization arrived in a mammoth caravan with multitudes of people along with their domesticated animals, and judging from their sheep, cattle, graylag geese, Scottish terrier and Bloodhound dogs, they most likely originated somewhere around the British Isles, Scotland or eastern Europe. They lived right 'here' in the middle of the North American continent, below and to the west of the last retreating glacier, scattered within shouting distance along this beautiful little river valley that I live along today. They lived on individual herd steads that were all part of a larger cohesive community that eventually had a centralized village near the fork in the river that's directly south of what was my grandpa's farm and which is one mile directly north of the small rural community of Ulysses, Nebraska. They had to have made it 'here' by moving east across all of what is now Russia. I can see where they could even have trekked across northern China.

For all we know, these people were world travelers and they could have split up and traveled anywhere that they wanted and would have looked like a force to be reckoned with as they boldly strode into a strange but already occupied land. The ones that went east eventually made it to the environmentally rich and plentiful volcanic Kamchatka Peninsula of Eastern Russia. Mind you, that it may not have been a peninsula then because sea levels were almost four hundred feet lower. They made it their coastal homeland from where they hunted humpback whales and sea lions until it went ballistic. The volcanic eruption that chased them away from it ejected huge amounts of ash, and that immense ash cloud caused them to move east out on to the ice sheet covered ocean of what is known today as the Pacific Ocean.

I keep thinking that it was the middle of the night when they were chased out of their beloved volcanic homeland but it may have been really dark because the volcanoes ash cloud was blocking out the sun, perhaps for days or weeks while they fled, and without the sun they had no idea which direction they were going. They unknowingly continued east until they realized that they were on the southern edge of the sheet of summertime sea ice so they kept going until they made landfall near what is now Washington State, all the while surviving on kelp and sea lions...and perhaps humpback whales because I'm sure that they brought their kayaks with them. They settled there until the next epic event forced them east again.

That epic event was a great flood that sent them trekking east again until they ended up in the middle of the North American continent below the last retreating glacier. It was the melting of that glacier that caused the epic flood that forced them out of Washington State in the first place and that continued to create the Channeled Scablands, most likely when Lake Missoula's glacial ice dam breached for the last time. The Mammoth People couldn't resist taking up residence in this nice little river valley that I call home and that at that time was in the middle of what today would seem like the Serengeti of Africa. This was the most peaceful place that they could find that didn't have any erupting volcanoes or lahars, no predator ice that they could unexpectedly fall through or glacial ice dams that could break and drown them. They had kayaks made from sea lion pelts that they used to spear breaching humpback whales along the southern edge of the ice sheet covered ocean. They also fashioned sea lion pelts into hooded parkas and other wearing apparel such as hats and gloves and leggings. The women had long wool dress skirts or coats. I have the Mammoth Peoples microlithic abstract art on flint and potsherds to back up this outlandish claim.

The cat figurine handle that's on one of the pottery rim sherds in my display cabinet that shows a kitty sitting on his haunches with his front paws on the rim of the pot 'is' a representation of the waist high young maidens kitty that's sitting on his haunches and grooming himself...or raising his paws up towards her for her to pick him up and carry him in the 'volcanic mass exodus' folklore tale, although the youngest Mammoth People children may have simply saw it as a kitty sitting on his haunches with his paws on top of the rim of the pot because it was full of fresh warm cow's milk...

The conclusions that I've come to after a lifetime of research is that the universal language will always be art……..how else could

I have possibly figured out the existence of the Mammoth People and the Palomino Pony People across all of the millennia? The deciphered Mammoth People hunter herder's microlithic abstract art figurative language is the 'latchkey' that unlocks and opens a portal into the stone-age past, back in time starting with the end of the Pleistocene. We'll be able to see how the Mammoth People looked and what their environment was like as far back as they used the microlithic abstract art figurative language 'starting' with the end of the Pleistocene epoch which was at the pinnacle of their microlithic abstract art figurative language skills and consequently was also when the abstract art figurative language was lost because none of the subsequent cultures artifacts has their art on it...or does it? It may very well have continued in Europe but it doesn't appear to have continued here in the center of the North American continent which leads me to conclude that they either died out, were eradicated by the Palomino Pony People warrior braves and civil war, or just maybe they possibly blended into the larger red skinned Indian nation after war decimated the Mammoth People's culture.

And let's not forget the asteroid impact theory.

I know that the Palomino Pony People didn't create art 'on' the flint and stone that they were using which explains why they have such perfectly symmetrical spears and prismatic knives that are highly sought after by collectors today. That's why their prismatic knives are so long and smooth surfaced and appealing to the eye. They didn't etch and rub them down into works of art like the Mammoth People did. They were excellent flint knappers but they didn't create art 'on' stone beyond the actual flute channel that they struck off of the base of their flint spear points. Their flint and stone tools were art unto itself but their real 'art' remained more organic meaning that they probably stuck to bone, wood, hide, pottery, textiles and feathers like the gruff chief's headdress. Consequently, the Mammoth People hunter herder's microlithic abstract art makes the production of a flute channel on a spear point's base look like child's play.

Before I figured out the entire Mammoth Peoples microlithic abstract art figurative language, I grappled with the assumption that these folks that created this microlithic abstract art were using some sort of small mechanical grinding wheel as absurd as that sounds. I'm assuming, it would have been physically operated by a second person while the artisan created his artwork but at this point I believe that it was real and I have many examples of the impression a small grinding wheel would make in stone, to verify it. Small circular impressions some with lips that would not have been possible to make by rubbing the stone by hand are on these pieces. If the Mammoth People were clever enough to create the microlithic abstract art, then they would have been clever enough to have created a rotary grinding wheel device (possibly out of fresh or green bone) that could have been powered by another person while the artist ground the heat treated flint against it, rapidly grinding out the simulacrum or pareidolia imagery that he perceived within it and possibly even grinding the whole outside side of the combined optical and cognitive illusion close-up image that the microlithic cognitive illusion reflection images are reflecting off of while also creating honed sharp knife edges so that the artwork could also be used as their utilitarian knife scraper eating utensil.

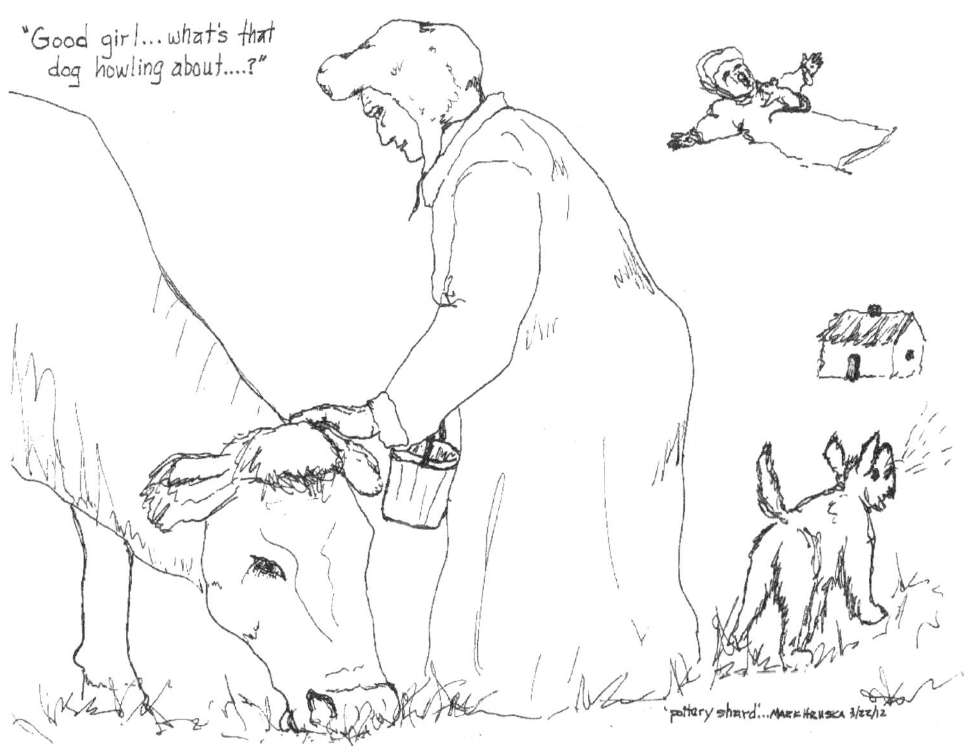

9. The pesky house rat took advantage of the time
that grandma spent away from the cottage when she had
to get fresh warm cow's milk for her crying infant grandchild.

Chapter Eight

What I've Learned

This chapter consists of musings that I've written down after having figured out the majority of the repetitive themes or folklore tales and after having 'seen' what I've seen on their microlithic abstract artworks through the eyes of the Mammoth People hunter herder microlithic abstract artisans who created them. Figuring out the Mammoth People hunter herder's microlithic abstract art figurative language is in itself a means to an end 'dismissing' all other archaeological processes simply because no one alive today could replicate what the Mammoth People were creating using cognitive and dexterity skills that required vision that was at least three times more acute then ours is today. We can only imagine how much more acute their sense of hearing and smell were. The art alone is a testimonial to their incredible cognitive and physical abilities. Collectively, the art from this one 'provenance' gives a complete picture of their lives along with the environment that they left behind when they left their erupting volcanic homeland and the new one that they settled in that had entirely new predators. The art also proves that the Mammoth People were global travelers and could cover vast distances over the course of one lifetime.

After more research on the subject of how the Mammoth People could have traveled to here from the Kamchatka Peninsula of Eastern Russia without having to go all of the way up across the Bearing Straight and that cold and inhospitable land, I came up with a much more plausible route as I described in an earlier chapter. To expand on that theory I would submit that you search the internet and look closely at the summertime and wintertime sea ice cover during the end of the last glaciation approximately twelve thousand years ago and you'll see that during the wintertime the Pacific sea ice was as far south as about the middle of the Kamchatka Peninsula stretching east across the Pacific Ocean to about southern California. In the summertime the sea ice cover extended to where the southern border of Washington State is today. Either way, if an erupting volcano in Kamchatka drove the Mammoth People out on the Pacific sea ice, they could have trekked in their long mammoth caravan along the southern edge of it all the way to Washington State. This would explain all of the repetitive themes of the Mammoth People falling through the predator ice and through the lightly frozen over sea lion breathe holes that were in it. They didn't walk on the much rougher glacial ice sheet at all. They walked on relatively smooth ice that obviously wasn't too thick in some places which would explain why sometimes parts of the mammoth caravan broke through it and other times it was just the fair young maiden who was riding her horse that broke through the predator ice that then closed back over them like a trap door drowning them.

Once the Mammoth People made it to the Washington State coastline they possibly settled there long enough to have built cottages and resumed a similar lifestyle that they had on the other side of the Pacific at Kamchatka. This included hunting humpback whales in their sea lion pelt covered kayaks. This all changed when the epic deluge that flowed west across the Channeled Scab Lands all the way to the Pacific coast swept them out of their new homes and maybe could have even swept them away while they were actually trekking across the midsection of Washington State. They kept going east because they knew that it was impossible to go back west across the treacherous predator ice and back to a mountainous land that could erupt at any time spitting fiery lava bombs and suffocating ash clouds that roar with thunderous white lightning bolts, and that also sends mud lahars sweeping down through the valleys and destroying everything. No, their best bet was to get past the mountain range that was to the east of them and keep going until they found a peaceful place to make a permanent home.

So they trekked on. They crossed the Rocky Mountain range where the great deluge originated, most likely walking right through the gorge where the immense glacial meltwater ice dam breached. This would have given them a good view of the inside side of the drained Lake Missoula and its shoreline strandlines that extended all the way to eastern Montana. This would have taken them across the gap between the two ice sheets and they simply would have followed the southern edge of the Laurentide Ice Sheet to where it curved southward which was about where the Missouri River starts to border north eastern Nebraska. The ice sheet dipped down to the southern part of the present day State of Iowa blocking any further eastward movement and forcing them southward. Eventually they ended up in a cozy little hydrologic river valley that was lush with prairie grass to feed their mammoth and cattle and that was plentiful with other wildlife. The drawback of course was the saber-toothed cats, lions, grizzly and short-faced bears and dire wolves that constantly stalked them and their domesticated animals, but the Mammoth People probably didn't realize that these predators wouldn't be their biggest worry. It turned out to be the Palomino Pony People....

The Mammoth People were the first Eurasians to explore the North American continent....not the Vikings who made it there twelve millennia later...although the Vikings ancestors may very well have been the Mammoth People. I would like nothing better than to try to trace the Mammoth Peoples culture through their microlithic abstract art by identifying it on artifacts found on the European continent.

The Mammoth People could have easily been called the Submissive Ewe People because that was their religion just like humans today call themselves Christians, Muslims or any other religion that believes in a mystical higher power. They occupied this area from where I conduct this research, for quite some time, possibly one hundred years or more. They started out by being spread out on herd steads along the river but eventually there was a good size community located at my sites of '1a', '1c' and '1d'. I have to ask, what makes archaeologists think that the Clovis People whom I'm confident were the Palomino Pony People, were the only culture that was here? The Mammoth People were exhausting the natural resources in the center of this continent which ultimately irritated the Palomino Pony People to the point that they revolted. Tensions built between the two cultures until all-out war broke out....the first 'civil war' on this continent. It's overwhelmingly evident which culture won that first civil war. The Palomino Pony People looked exactly the same way to the second wave of Caucasian Pioneers that trekked across this continent more recently with their oxen pulled covered wagons and wagon trains, as they did to the Mammoth People all of those millennia ago. The only difference was that they exclusively rode the supposedly extinct Sulphur or Palomino breed of horse when the first wave of Caucasians trekked here in their long mammoth caravan that contained multitudes of Caucasian trekkers and their domesticated animals that included mammoths that were pulling big enclosed but topless wooden sleds that would float like a boat when crossing rivers.

I got to thinking about why all of the horses from the

Pleistocene were technically referred to as Sulphur which had the hide colors of a Palomino horse; golden with white facial markings, white legging markings and sometimes a white mane and white tail. It occurred to me that if horses were evolving alongside lions and saber-toothed cat predators, wouldn't it make sense for the horses hide to match the color of a lions hide so that lions wouldn't see them as easily or would simply mistake them for another tawny yellow colored lion or a saber-toothed cat? The white diamond shaped pattern on the palomino's face would also look like the white hair that's on a male lion's chin. The last thing that a prey animal would want is to have a flashy hide pattern or a color that stood out. Even in a snowy environment the horse's head and back would be somewhat camouflaged when a predator looked towards it because its face and the mane hair on the nape of its neck as well as its tail and feet would be white like patches of snow that are surrounded by golden or tan and would simply blend in with the winter time prairie grass that has patches of snow in it.

The prehistoric culture that occupied my '2a' site that the archaeologists at the University of Nebraska call the 'Central Plains Tradition' and that they claim were the ancestors of the Pawnee, are in fact the Paleo Amerind Mammoth People culture. So wherever they find similar artifacts that include the potsherds and especially the thumb scraper or end scrapers that have graver spurs on both sides of the widest rounded end, it will most definitely be associated with the Mammoth People because every one of those thumb scrapers are the 'predator's bent forelegs featuring the prey they're stalking' art form and they definitely have a predator prey theme on them. Museum archives, especially here in eastern Nebraska, are no doubt full of Mammoth People microlithic abstract art that's waiting to be brushed clean with a toothbrush and water and be interpreted.

I've probably mentioned this earlier, but I thought I better make sure that it's stated in clearer terms. It involves how you position the 'rotational change-up' microlithic abstract artworks when you view a particular image or scene. You are positioned to view the piece the way that the hunter herder, the headmaster of a school or his student microlithic abstract artisans intend, when the ends of your fingers fit into the nicely rubbed out concave crescent shaped edges of the flint artwork or when one of the straight edges of the flint artwork are horizontal or vertical to your gaze. If you do that when you first view the piece, you'll be set up to see the first image or scene of the folklore tale. Either way, no matter which image or scene you see first on the 'rotational change-up' artwork, you'll eventually come full circle and will have seen all of the scenes even if you jumped into the middle of the folklore tale with the first image or scene that's apparent to you and that most likely drew you into the storyline. When I write up a piece I usually save the most mind bending image or scene which usually is a fantastic combined optical and cognitive illusion close-up image, for last in an effort to leave the viewer with the greatest mind altering effect. Possibly the way that grandpa would leave on his grandchild as he told one of the frightening or riveting folklore tales that perhaps involved the pack of hungry dire wolves chasing the ox pulled sled that has mom herdswoman mushing it while her two daughters hang on to the front wall of the sled screaming for their lives. If there are several fantastic close-up images, I will use a gripping one at the beginning of the piece to draw the viewer into the storyline and conclude with a mind bending one that will warp the viewer's perception of time....

Let me give you another example of what the Mammoth People hunter herder microlithic abstract art is...... I compare interpreting the Mammoth People hunter herder microlithic abstract art figurative language to reading 'Braille'. It's so foreign to our way of perception especially if you read normally with both of your eyes, nonetheless Braille gives its blind reader the perfect imagery that the writer wants them to see in their 'mind's eye'. So too, the hunter herder microlithic abstract artist creates a whole story, not from what your fingers touch across the pages of a 'book' or from what your eyes read on the pages of a book, but from what your fingers touch and what your eyes read around a tiny stone....a 'microlith'. Instead of reading literal written words you're reading a figurative imagery that makes up individual images and scenes that when combined compose a repetitive theme...or an Ice Age storytellers folklore tale.

`The waist high young maiden and her soaking wet kitty are lovingly reaching for each other and anticipating their embrace!'

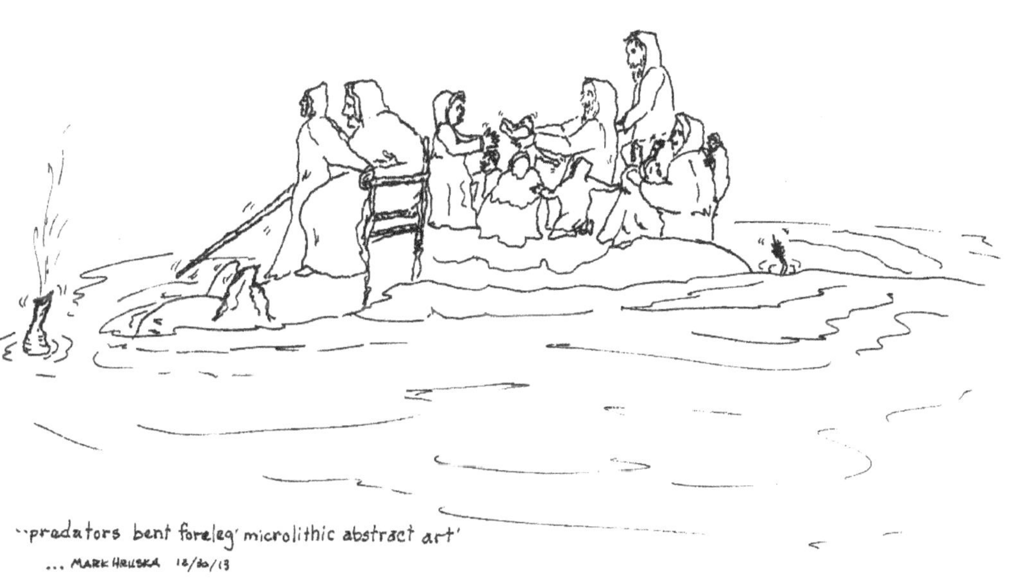

10. Concentrating grandma is steering the
submerged swimming lead mammoth after they rescued
the entire lead family…after the 'epic deluge' swept them away.

Chapter Nine

Complete Stories of Some of the Most Popular Folklore Tales

This chapter is long but I felt it my duty to the Mammoth People culture to convey their complete folklore tales to the best of my abilities in order to be fair to them and the fantastic microlithic abstract artworks that they created. You are welcome to skip ahead to the following chapters and then come back to finish these folklore tales later, but I strongly suggest to work your way through them to get the best understanding of their world before moving on to the rest of the book. As with chapter six, you can take frequent breaks to give these stories time to digest.

This is the complete story of one of the most popular Mammoth People's repetitive themes or folklore tales that I'm sure grandpa enjoyed telling to his grandchildren and that I call the 'sorceress'. It centers on the elderly hunter herdsman or 'grandpa' and it was of when he took his bloodhound pup out on a leash to train him so that he could help herd the cattle and the mammoth. They're in a mountainous environment and when they get tuckered out they laid down to take a nap. Grandpa rests the back of his hood covered head against some rocks while his bent knees are together up off the ground and the bloodhound pup rests his chin on the top of his feet. A pair of nesting black viper snakes is under the rocks that grandpa is resting his head on. One of them comes out and bites him on the neck or face while he snoozes. In some cases he makes it back to the cottage before the venom makes him delirious and eventually renders him unconscious...but in others, the pup howls until the other family members come to find them because it's getting dusk.

One of the elderly hunter herdsman's family members, usually his fair young maiden granddaughter or his teenage young lad grandson, takes their horse and goes fetch the sorceress and her three chanting assistants. The sorceress recites incantations while she wafts ceremonial smoke over grandpa's supine body that's laying on a cot or bed in front of the fireplace. She continues to waft the smoke over unconscious grandpa's white bearded face while her three chanting assistants chant and bow in homage to the Steller's sea eagle spirit that they're summoning. The three chanting assistants stand abreast of each other on the opposite side of grandpa's cot from the sorceress. The rest of the family is waiting, watching and listening intently to all of the incantations and ritual from just inside the front door of the quaint cottage or from outside of the cottage's Dutch door and shutter covered windows where they peer through into the smoke filled room. Grandma is the one that's usually standing right inside of the cottage's Dutch doors doorway with her arms holding one or two of her waist high rambunctious grandsons close in front of her. Her left hand can often be seen on one of their left shoulders or across their chest. Her concerned fair young maiden granddaughter's petite face and bonnet covered head can usually be seen on the other side of her which would be to the right of her.

When the sorceress wafts enough of the smoke over the elderly hunter herdsman's unconscious face he sputters and coughs back to life, most likely from the suffocating smoke rather than actually having been rid of the venomous snake spirit that the Steller's sea eagle spirit drove out of his slumbering body. Through it all the loyal bloodhound pup stays by grandpa's side with his head resting near grandpa's head or near his feet, usually over them like they were when they were napping together on their hike. He's protecting his master from the big black Steller's sea eagle spirit that's flapping her wings over the two of them which makes her ponder how loyal the pup is when the old 'coot' could have easily gotten them both killed, not to mention that she's out in the Pleistocene night reciting incantations when she has better things to do, and how are she and the three chanting assistants going to get home without getting eaten by hungry dire wolves? This would no doubt put the irate look on her face that's encompassed by the black tight fitting garment. The sorceress is wearing a long black cape that covers her arms so that when she spreads them wide apart she appears to have wings that can flap the smoke over the unconscious supine elderly hunter herdsman's face. She wears a black tight fitting head garment that encompasses her face from above her eyebrows to under her chin. Her three chanting assistants are wearing the same tight fitting head garment and stand abreast of each other while they chant the incantations.

When the sorceress is standing with her black cloak covered arms spread wide apart and up shoulder high, she reminds me of the fighting Steller's sea eagle that would have inhabited the Mammoth Peoples homeland of the Kamchatka Peninsula of Eastern Russia. The Steller's sea eagle spirit would not be afraid of the venomous black viper snake. When it is victorious after winning a fight it postures in a very similar fashion to the sorceress when she wafts the smoke forward with her extended black cape covered arms...or wings. The Steller's sea eagles huge whitish yellow beak goes right up to its eyes which makes it look like the sorceress's face that's encompassed by a black tight fitting head garment, which would symbolize the Steller's sea eagle spirit's black feather covered head. Even when it spreads its wings it has a horizontal white streak on the leading edges of them that looks like a herdswoman's arms that have a white undergarment with the black cape draped over them. When the wings are down, it looks like it has white shoulder patches. The resemblances of the fierce bird's markings and the sorceress's attire are uncanny. At some point, she's flapping her wings and looking up into the smoke filled ceiling of the gabled roof that has wooden ceiling rafters running across it, as if she's looking up into the cloudy heavens to summon the Steller's sea eagle spirit. When she does, she comes face to face with a pair of coughing and choking rats that are clinging to the underside of the wooden ceiling rafter and trying to get their sniffing noses as low as possible into the smoke filled cottage to get a breath of fresher air. They don't go unnoticed by the waist high young maiden's kitty that she's always holding which alerts her to their unwanted presence too.

A slight variation that I've found to this repetitive theme involves the coughing and choking rats. What I found on a couple of other pieces is that instead of being on top of the wooden ceiling rafters of the cottage that the exorcism ceremony is taking place in, the coughing and choking rats are in a hole on the end of the wooden mantle shelf above the fireplace. This new variation in the repetitive theme has given me a new perspective of the inside of the Mammoth Peoples cottages. We even get to see the end of the peg that's holding the right end of the wooden mantel shelf to the sod cottages wall or to the stone that's above the fireplace. Personally, I think that the chimney was just built from sod like the rest of the cottage and limestone was used for the hearth. The gabled roofs were definitely covered with thatch of some kind and in this part of the world I can see where cattail leaves would have made great thatch for the Mammoth Peoples gabled roofs...that the rats would have loved to make their home in too...

Another Mammoth People hunter herder microlithic abstract artist's repetitive theme or folklore tale is one that dwelt on the teenage young lad's desire to impress a fair young maiden but ultimately ended up disappointing his grandpa because he was trying too hard to impress the fair young maiden. This is the folklore tale that I call the 'bull rider' and it's of a Pleistocene bull riding rodeo. I kid you not. The premise of the folklore tale is that the teenage young lad rider is trying to impress a fair young maiden in the crowd of spectators and must have gotten thrown in short order. The bucking bull threw him so violently that he was jerked clean out of his sea lion pup pelt boots. He flew so high that you could see ducks flying by further behind or on the other side of him near the top of his head which also meant that it was most likely late fall at the time of the annual Chautauqua type gathering. The rodeo allowed the young Pleistocene cattle rustlers to show off their cattle handling and bull riding skills that they had sharpened throughout the long spring and summer months when they herded their cattle and mammoth to the best patches of prairie grass.

When the thrown teenage young lad picks himself up and dusts himself off, he bends over to retrieve his summertime leather cap and his two sea lion pup pelt boots but while doing so he glances over towards the crowd to see, not the fair young maiden who he was trying to impress and who was embarrassingly leaving the stands, but his extremely disappointed elderly hunter herder grandpa who's turning his head away in disgust. He and grandma are getting up to go home while the sun drops low in the afternoon autumn sky.

This is a description of the 'most common' of the Mammoth People hunter herder microlithic abstract artist's repetitive themes. I should say that it is the most common 'version' of the volcanic homeland ones that involve erupting volcanoes because there are also volcanic eruption themes of lahars sweeping through the valley that the Mammoth People lived in and they roar through like a pair of attacking lions that swept away the whole village. Then there are pieces with the theme of the erupting volcanoes roaring male lion ash cloud belching out fiery cinder balls or lava bombs that fly over the fleeing trekker's heads as they climb the steep mountainous terrain and it's of when the trekkers are the closest to the erupting volcano that they are fleeing. The most common and number one version of the volcanic repetitive themes though is the one that I refer to as the 'volcanic mass exodus'. It's of when the Mammoth Peoples ancestors were chased out of their beloved homeland by a violently erupting volcano and its pursuing broiling lightning filled ash cloud that chased them like a roaring male lion that threatened to pounce on them. Sometimes his lioness mate is beside him but he usually sent her ahead in the form of screaming white hot lava bombs that scorched the poor fleeing trekkers. The thunderously roaring male lion ash cloud had lightning flashing out of his head and out the ends of his pouncing foreleg's front paws. As I just mentioned, he occasionally sent his pouncing lioness mate screaming towards the trekkers in the form of a white hot fiery cinder ball or lava bomb that flew over the multitudes of Mammoth People trekker's heads like incoming meteors that had tails.

Crotchety grandma is sitting on her special armchair that's attached to a stretcher and being carried by four porters on their shoulders. Normally, she's sitting on her special armchair atop the lead mammoth but the mountainous terrain is so steep that porters have to carry her in order to keep her level. The front left porter is always her teenage young lad grandson and he's standing abreast to the left of his stern dad who is always the front right one. Delirious grandpa is laying back on a travois that's being pulled by the 'beast of burden' horse. This positions his head near the rear end of the horse and he's always looking behind the trekkers and up at the broiling ash cloud that's pursuing them and that they're fleeing. It's the middle of the Pleistocene night and everything that's seen in this repetitive theme is being seen by the flashes of light from the lightning that's coming out of the ash cloud which is why delirious grandpa thinks he's seeing a huge roaring male lion that's about to pounce on him up in the broiling ash cloud, and that the lightning is coming from within its opened mouth that's roaring thunderously.

The sweet considerate waist high young maiden goes over to the right side of her delirious grandpa's head to try to understand what he's ranting about as he points skyward towards the broiling ash cloud that's above them. She shouts at her stern dad and her teenage big brother who are crotchety grandma's front right and front left porters, to hold up and that's when crotchety grandma tells them to turn around and bring her back alongside of the right side of delirious grandpa so that she can have a loud discussion with him to see what he's ranting about. When they do, the front left porter who is the teenage young lad will be standing behind his little sister to the left side of delirious grandpa's travois which is to the right side of delirious grandpa's feet. In this manner crotchety grandma can lean over the left arm of her special armchair and have a very loud discussion with her delirious elderly husband about what they should do now since the roaring male lion that they both think that they see up in the broiling ash cloud, seems to be overtaking them and about to pounce on them. This shifts most of crotchety grandma's weight onto the teenager's sore right shoulder and makes him feel like the 'beast of burden' that he sees when he looks back to his left on past his little sister at the 'beast of burden' horse's head as it struggles to get it over or under the left travois pole so that he can turn his head sharply around and back to his left to see and hear what grandpa's ranting about behind him.

During crotchety grandma and delirious grandpa's loud discussion there's a bright flash of white lightning from the male lion ash cloud followed by a thunderous roar. This frightens the waist high young maiden's kitty that she's always holding near her chest and causes him to bolt from her arms on to her delirious grandpa's face scratching or biting it and making him more delirious than he already was because he thinks that he's seeing the roaring male lion ash clouds face as close up as he just saw the frightened kitty's face. This in turn makes crotchety grandma even more irritated sending her into a conniption fit releasing a relentless tirade on her mortified waist high young maiden granddaughter at the end of which she points out in front of her to where she wants the now sobbing waist high young maiden to go 'march' so that she can keep a glaring eyeball on her and her naughty kitty. On her way to march out in front of her big brother and stern dad the sobbing waist high young maiden stops briefly in front of her compassionate big brother and lays her forehead against his chest for sympathy and reassurance. He softly speaks the words of encouragement that she so desperately needs to hear before she turns away from the front of him to start 'madly marching' out ahead of him towards the multitudes of other miserable weary trekkers who have split around the dysfunctional lead family that was held up in the middle of a narrow windy mountain pass.

Once his upset little sister and her naughty kitty leave the front of him, the disgusted teenager turns to his right towards his stern dad who's standing abreast to the right of him and yells at him questioning why he doesn't do something about crotchety grandma to get her to quit yelling at his poor sweet innocent little sister. At this point I have to mention that one of the reasons that crotchety grandma who is normally so kind and loving but is now so irritable, is because an incoming screaming white hot fiery lioness cinder ball or lava bomb has landed on the top of one of her gnarled hands that's cringing as it grasps the end of the arm of her special armchair. The white hot fiery lioness cinder ball or lava bomb is scorching a deep burn into the top of it at the same time that she's yelling at her sobbing waist high young maiden granddaughter to go 'march' out ahead of her big brother and her dad where she can keep one glaring eyeball on her and the other one on her naughty kitty.

When she looks at the cinder ball that's scorching a deep burn on the top of her cringing old hand she sees the lioness cinder ball as a lioness that has just made a kill and is sitting on her haunches with her back to grandma. She's looking back over her left shoulder while her scorching paws hold down her prey which is crotchety grandma's gnarled hand, and her lioness eyes have that look that's telling grandma what she's thinking which is...'all mine'.

Meanwhile, all stern dad wants to do is get his family as far away from the violently erupting volcano and its pursuing ash cloud as possible before the broiling ash cloud overtakes them and suffocates them all to death. When I say his family, I haven't explained where mom and the infant are in relation to everyone else. As the caravan moves along, the mammoth that normally carries grandma and her special armchair on her back, is still being led by dad and she follows along to the right and slightly behind him. You have to remember that the front right stretcher pole that grandma's special armchair is attached to, is being carried on dads left shoulder. The mammoth doesn't require a rein and she naturally follows her lead hunter herder just by sniffing where he is with her 'fishing' trunk tip. Dad's right hand isn't free though, it's hanging on to the domestic milk cow's rein strap that's also leading her and she is carrying his infant that's strapped to a backboard and slung over her left shoulder....his hands are always full.

The story doesn't end here though for you see, after the upset waist high young maiden leaves the front of her compassionate big brother to 'madly march' out in front of him and rejoin the ranks of other miserable weary Mammoth People trekkers who are trudging along to the left of the dysfunctional lead family that is held up in the middle of the narrow windy mountain pass, she encounters another mortifying problem all because she decides to take out her own disgust for being treated so unfairly by her crotchety grandma, on her naughty kitty as he briskly walks along to one side of her. She's 'madly marching' along taking big marching steps while she swings her little arms wildly to and fro with her red cape blowing out behind her bonnet covered head, and she's looking down towards her meowing kitty as he briskly walks along beside her while she scolds him telling him that she's not going to carry him no matter how much he complains because of all of that trouble that he's gotten her into with crotchety grandma. The trouble was that she was paying no attention to where she was madly marching to and she unexpectedly ran into a poor old decrepit herdswoman who was trudging along leaning on her cane. The elderly decrepit herdswoman was already on her last leg and when she fell down she more or less hit the ground dead making the poor waist high young maiden's plight that much more miserable ....giving credence to all of the Mammoth People children that were listening to the folklore tale, of how absolutely horrible that would have been to have gone through, and what their ancestors had to have endured in order for them to get to 'here'.....

After having gone through a great deal of the baked stone or heat treated stone artifacts, I've come to the conclusion that practically every single one of them no matter the size or shape, has imagery on them from the 'volcanic mass exodus' folklore tale. Most common are the optical illusion close-up images of the heads of the sobbing waist high young maiden, her empathetic big brother who is crotchety grandma's front left porter, crotchety grandma and delirious grandpa. Sometimes you get stern dad who is crotchety grandma's front right porter and sometimes you'll see the 'beast of burden' horse that the compassionate teenage young lad feels like when he sees him struggling to turn his head and try to get it under the left travois pole to see and hear what delirious grandpa is ranting about behind him. You'll also see the frightened kitty's face, but no image is more replicated than the 'mortified', 'sobbing' or 'madly marching' waist high young maiden's pug nosed childlike face and her bonnet covered head that has a windblown red cape hood over it and that reminds me of our own 'Little Red Riding Hood' character that is portrayed in our childhood fairytales. Sometimes I find imagery of a ribbon tied around the bonnet like a headband that's behind its frilled front edge and that wraps around her head puffing up the top of the bonnet. The 'volcanic mass exodus' repetitive theme was almost like a religion to the Mammoth People that honored their ancestors for the incredibly arduous trials and tribulations that they went through to get to 'here' starting with the violently erupting volcano that chased them out of their beloved homeland in a mass exodus. The erupting volcanoes' broiling ash cloud that delirious grandpa and crotchety grandma saw an attacking roaring male lion with lightning coming out of its eyes and opened mouth in, drove them out on to the predator ice sheet and the rest is prehistoric history.

I have interpreted several pieces that have a common repetitive theme that involves a stalking saber-toothed cat that's lurking in the tall prairie grass. The lead hunter herder is trying to locate him per the instructions from his very agitated elderly mother who's sitting on her special armchair atop the nervous lead mammoth that the lead hunter herder is leading. She's usually leaning out to the left side of the nervous lead mammoth hanging out over the left arm of her special armchair as she points to where she swears that she last saw the big cat lurking. The lead hunter herder is to the left and slightly in front of the nervous lead mammoth's head and he is seen turning towards the mammoth and his agitated elderly mother for directions so that he can find the lurking saber-toothed cat and prod it out of its hiding place. He is shown holding his spear out in front of him pointed down towards the tall swaying prairie grass where the nervous lead mammoth and agitated grandma absolutely know the saber-toothed cat is lurking.

In other versions of this folklore tale, the waist high young lad is out in front of the nervous lead mammoth with his dad but he's overly confident and comes face to face with either a lurking saber-toothed cat or a male lion or a lioness. Dad usually is close enough behind him to jab his spear in their face before they pounce on the inexperienced waist high young lad.

In another scenario, the fair young maiden is riding her palomino horse out to the left of the nervous lead mammoth and her agitated grandmother and she's such an overachiever that she thought that she would go further out ahead of her lead hunter dad to help him locate the lurking saber-toothed cat or lion that her agitated grandma knows she saw lurking out in the tall swaying prairie grass. The trouble was that she was so overly eager and confident that she got too far out ahead of her lead hunter herder dad who had a big spear, and in more than one instance she was pounced on and taken cleanly off of her palomino horse. If a saber-toothed cat attacked her it usually bit her head clean off...leaving her agitated grandma stunned speechless.... The lesson for the overly eager fair young maidens that the folklore tale was being told to was to be cautious no matter how overly confident and safe you felt with your new found maturity.

I've interpreted many pieces that involve the Mammoth People's 'summertime picnic' which was a very large gathering of all of the Mammoth People families and their pets from the surrounding herd steads. The main theme of the piece is that a pair of dire wolves, a pair of lions or a pair of rogue male lions, or a saber-toothed cat attacks the multitudes of frightened and horrified picnic goers that scatter and stampede towards the exit or gate where the horses and mammoth are standing tied to the 'hitching post'. Some of the rides are harnessed to sleds or travoises and all of them are agitated with the horses rearing up as the crowd of screaming fleeing picnicker's stampedes towards them.

In the repetitive theme that shows the pair or pack of dire wolves attacking the fleeing picnickers, one of them singles out a petrified waist high young lad and is face to face with him while the waist high young lad's ferocious Scottie stands between them to try to ward off the attack. He holds the dire wolf at bay until either grandma or grandpa hobbles up and whacks the dire wolf over the head with their cane. On one piece that I interpreted, it was grandpa that ultimately saved his waist high young lad grandson and then there are scenes of him leaning on his waist high young lad grandson's right shoulder with his right arm while his left one leaned on his cane. Both of their faces were bloodied because they were mauled by the dire wolf. The waist high young lad was helping his injured grandpa get to the exit where their nervous mare was waiting for him with the travois harnessed to her. She had her head down and to her right under the right travois pole to try to see why everyone was screaming and shouting while they stampeded towards her. There's this combined optical and cognitive illusion close-up image of her and then there's a closer-up one that's more of a front view of her that still has her head lowered to get under the right travois pole. This piece is titled 3/23/13... 'prismatic knife'... 'Injured grandpa was helped to his travois and the waiting mare by his grandson after beating the dire wolf that mauled them over the head with his cane.'

These summertime picnics, teen dances, rodeos or wedding themes that have a lot or multitudes of Mammoth People in attendance are usually on the heat treated fossiliferous flint because so many of the round and oval fossils that are embedded in the heat treated flint look exactly like microlithic cognitive illusion images of heads and faces of the Mammoth People. They're complete with bonnets or hoods and you can see the features of their faces including eyes, mouths, beards and mustaches. Don't ask me how the hunter herder microlithic abstract artists did it but they usually created the entire repetitive theme around one distinct microlithic image by rubbing or etching them out and then creating an optical or a combined optical and cognitive illusion close-up image to go with it that they're reflecting off of...such as one side of the attacking dire wolf's head. Many of these pieces have multiple optical and cognitive illusion close-up images though and as you turn the 'rotational change-up' art form to the next one you will have more reflection images reflecting off of that next close-up image. This could be on the exact same side of the stone.

In other words, you could look at one side of the piece and see the combined optical and cognitive illusion close-up image of the left side view of a fleeing herdswoman's bonnet covered head and face that has many microlithic cognitive illusion reflection images reflecting off of it of other fleeing picnickers and even the dire wolves that are jumping up on them and attacking them. Then you could rotate her head upside down or invert it and it will morph into the combined optical and cognitive illusion close-up image of the right side view of her waist high young maiden daughter's bonnet covered head and screaming face that she's pulling along as they flee together. This makes the mother and daughter's heads inverted 'opposing heads' because they share the same backs of their bonnet covered heads.....and their faces, and they're at odds with each other because the mother has to pull her daughter along. They could just as easily have their faces on each side of this side of the stone and even though they would be looking away from each other in opposite directions, you would actually be seeing them in your 'mind's eye' as 'face to face' according to the Mammoth People microlithic abstract art 'rules'. They would still be 'opposing heads' because they would share the same backs of their heads or bonnets meaning that they would be 'in' each other's heads thinking or experiencing the same horrific moment in Pleistocene time knowing how the other thinks and feels. All around this side of the screaming waist high young maiden's bonnet and face will be more microlithic cognitive illusion reflection images including a reflection image of her mother that will give you an exact idea of where she is in relationship to herself.

This is true of how you would see a reflection of the waist high young maiden that's reflecting off of mom herdswoman's combined optical and cognitive illusion close-up image. If they're looking straight at each other you will most likely see a reflection of the screaming waist high young maiden's face off of mom's chin, unless mom is being shoved down to the ground by one of the attacking dire wolves that are jumping up on the back of her head and shoulders. Then you may see the reflection of her screaming waist high young maiden daughter's horrified face on the side of her face as she falls forward in front of her. Eventually, you get the whole theme put together in you 'mind's eye' and it couldn't seem more real to you then if you saw a picture of it because you are actually seeing it in three dimensions like you would in real life, not two dimensions like you'd see on a flat sheet of paper that the picture is on. When you see the combined optical illusion close-up image of the front right side view or whatever view of the attacking snarling dire wolf, it leaves the most incredible 'indelible' impression in your 'mind's eye' that you'll swear that you just saw an attacking dire wolf from the Pleistocene because you are seeing it from the perspective of whoever was being attacked at that moment in time.

That goes for the 'indelible' impression that all of the other big attacking predators such as saber-toothed cats, lions or bears leave on your 'mind's eye'. Sometimes the predator isn't an animal at all, sometimes it's the face of the 'whooping and hollering' Palomino Pony People warrior brave when he's chasing the running and screaming fair young maiden from atop his 'running like the wind' palomino horse. The frightened fair young maiden looks to her right over her right shoulder and sees the close-up image of the left side view of the galloping horses wide eyed face right next to hers. Or she looks back over her right shoulder and the whooping and hollering warrior braves face is right above her right shoulder because he's leaning so far forward to the left side of his galloping horse's neck and mane. Now do you see.....?

One of the other versions of the 'summertime picnic' is of when a saber-toothed cat raids the picnic causing the same kind of chaos. In this version, he seems to be the only one and he stands in the middle of the large scattering crowd of fleeing picnickers and singles out the plumpest juiciest ones for his own picnic lunch which is usually the obese herdswoman mother and her obese son or daughter or both, who can't run as fast as the other leaner picnickers. You'll usually get scenes of the snarling saber-toothed cat turning to his left to look back behind him towards the petrified prey that he's guarding and claiming for his own while the fronts of their horrified images reflect off of the outside side of his long top left saber fang. The reflections of prey victims reflecting off of the predators exposed fangs is a common hunter herder microlithic abstract art practice. Depending on if a reflection is reflecting off of the front, the sides or even the 'inside' side of the exposed fang, you know exactly where the prey victim is located in relation to the predator's head. Sometimes the same exposed fang can represent the left or the right fang depending on what's reflecting off of it and in which 'scene' of the interpretation it's in.

When I finished the interpretation that I called 12/21/13... 'bifacial backed knife'... 'Grandpa's holding his granddaughter close while their horse struggles to see the mating lions that are oblivious to the loud powwow that's taking place below them.', I finished the lengthiest interpretation to that date because it was produced by a truly gifted Mammoth People hunter herder microlithic 'master' abstract artisan. He combined imagery that I've seen on two separate versions of the repetitive themes of the 'powwow' in order to show a more complete picture of the 'powwow' repetitive theme. For the first time I understood completely why the fair young maiden is running towards the lead hunter herder or 'dad' who's standing in front of the nervous lead mammoth while a whooping and hollering warrior brave chases her on his galloping palomino horse. When the raiding war party of whooping and hollering Palomino Pony People warrior braves ran circles around the Mammoth People mammoth caravan on their galloping palomino horses they spooked the fair young maiden's horse that was also pulling grandpa's travois and it took off running. The fair young maiden got thrown off because her dress covered legs had to straddle both of the travois poles that ran up along either side of the spooked horse. Grandpa bounced off of the travois because if it was too hard for the fair young maiden to stay on the running horse it was clearly too bumpy for grandpa to stay on the bouncing travois. He picked himself up and pulled the horse blanket that was covering him when he was comfortably riding on the travois, over his injured bald head and over his shoulders and cursed profanely as he hobbled in towards the powwow that was waiting to take place between the lead hunter herder or 'dad' and the gruff chief, in front of the nervous lead mammoth. The spooked horse ran with his empty travois towards the front of the nervous lead mammoth and stood next to the gruff chief and the lead hunter herder or 'dad' while a single whooping and hollering warrior brave chased in the screaming fair young maiden on his galloping palomino horse.

When the panting fair young maiden got up to the powwow, her irate grandma instructed her to hold her mesmerized little brother close to the front of her and stand right next to their dad because he had a big spear. When injured cursing grandpa hobbled up to the powwow, the panting fair young maiden left the side of her dad and her little brother who was mesmerized with the gruff chief's ridiculous wardrobe, and ran over to assist her injured grandpa. On this particular piece it was all being reflected off of a pair of obliviously mating lions that were up on a ledge above the scene and very close, usually over to the right of the nervous lead mammoth which was to the right of irate grandma who's sitting on her special armchair atop her. (To the right would be as if you were viewing the nervous lead mammoth from the rear.)

There are at least five versions of the repetitive 'powwow' theme. What I just mentioned happens in one of them. In a second version, the thrown and screaming fair young maiden who's running towards her dad at the front of the nervous lead mammoth that's carrying grandma on her special armchair atop her, is carrying her kitty in her right arm while her left hand holds up her long dress skirt so that she doesn't trip over it. As she runs screaming for her life towards her dad, her bonnet blows back exposing her long blond hairs pigtails. The whooping and hollering warrior brave's face is right behind her head as he leans as far forward as possible along the left side of his galloping palomino horse's neck. At some point when the fair young maiden's frightened kitty had had enough, he hissed and swiped at the galloping horse's wide opened left eye that was right next to the running fair young maiden's right elbow and shoulder. This caused the galloping horse to abruptly lower his head and apply the brakes which sent his whooping and hollering rider sailing over his head. His neck got tangled in the rein straps and when the slack ran out the sudden jerk broke his neck before his whooping and hollering mouth bit the Pleistocene dust. Sometimes his head is shown with a dent in it implying that he hit some rocks causing instant death, either way his body ends up prone on the Pleistocene prairie's windblown grass in front of his horse that instantly starts to nervously graze on the grass because he can't go anywhere since his dead rider is tangled in his rein straps.

The shocked and panting fair young maiden stands near the nervously grazing palomino horse's left shoulder because her irate grandma was yelling at her to stay right there while she quickly dismounted the nervous lead mammoth and spryly made her way out to the scene of the incident. The panting fair young maiden sat her golden kitty on the ground next to her where he sat on his haunches and kept his eyes glued on the nervously grazing golden palomino horses wide opened left eye that he almost clawed seconds earlier which had caused the galloping horse to apply the brakes, because he wanted to make sure that he didn't try anything else. When irate grandma got out to the scene of the incident, she immediately went to work untangling the fine animal's reins straps from around his dead rider's neck so that she could claim him for her fair young maiden granddaughter to ride instead of the one that pulled grandpa's travois. When bent over irate grandma finished untangling the rein straps and after having to turn the dead warrior brave over on to his back, she spit on his war painted white face which caused his horse to jerk away from her and rear up. He didn't pull the rein straps out of her hands though because she was clenching them tightly.

Meanwhile, aggravated cursing grandpa had finally made his way to the scene of the incident after having picked himself up and after draping the windblown horse blanket over his injured bald head and over his shoulders. When he got to where the dead warrior brave lay supine with his war painted white face facing skyward with irate grandma's spit already on it, pissed off cursing grandpa spread apart the windblown horse blanket, took out his penis and urinated on the supine dead warrior brave's war painted white face while his abhorrent fair young maiden granddaughter watched from up close. But further away the lead family and the gruff chief also watched the two elderly people desecrate the dead warrior brave's war painted white face while abhorrent mom herdswoman had to try to explain to their inquisitive waist high young maiden daughter why they were doing it. This all took place while the further back Mammoth People trekkers were making their way forward and gathering around the nervous lead mammoth and the powwow that was waiting to take place between dad and the gruff chief, after things were supposed to have settled down.

In the third version of the 'powwow' we see the mesmerized waist high young lad standing slightly to the right and in front of his lead hunter herder dad while his still panting big sister stands behind him and holds him close to the front of her. The crazy whooping and hollering warrior brave has just finished chasing her up to her lead hunter dad in front of the nervous lead mammoth while irate grandma was shrieking out instructions to everyone, mostly to her two grandchildren. The mesmerized waist high young lad stared in disbelief at the gruff chief's wardrobe that consisted of sea lion pup pelt flippers that hung down from his eagle feather headdresses' headband and dangled in the Pleistocene prairie wind against the sides of his gruff looking face. The frightened panting fair young maiden stared at the crazy warrior brave that had just chased her and who remained sitting on his high horse behind and to the left of the gruff chief. He was making weird facial gestures from atop his palomino horse that was standing alongside to the left of the gruff chief's nervously grazing palomino horse. The taunting warrior brave's jeering facial gestures that are only seen on this repetitive theme of the microlithic abstract art, is of him with a huge fake grinning smile that exposes as many of his front bright white teeth as possible to the frightened panting fair young maiden, which really irritates her grandma who's basically sitting straight across from him face to face because they're both sitting atop their rides at a higher vantage point.

At some point the gruff chief's fine palomino horse that had its head lowered to the ground and nervously grazing right in front of the mesmerized waist high young lad, started snorting and jerking his head up and down while he looked to his upper left which was to the mesmerized waist high young lad's upper right. When the waist high young lad looked up to his upper right he saw what the irritated snorting horse saw. It was a majestic male lion that was lounging in front of his den with his cubs up on the rock ledge. Sometimes the majestic male lion is mating with his lioness mate, either way it was an astounding sight to see for the waist high young lad and as hard as he might try, he just couldn't get anybody else to look where he was pointing to his upper right. After much excited persuasion, he finally got the gruff chief to look up towards the rock ledge and the majestic male lion after which dad and everyone else finally looked including the other trekkers who had gathered around the powwow with their backs to the rock ledge. Many times you'll see the majestic male lion lying on his belly with his forelegs out in front of him and his head erect much like the sphinx. He's licking off one of his front paws after having finished a big prey meal of what was most likely golden horse. When you zoom in, you'll see the microlithic cognitive illusion further away reflection image of the powwow with the excited waist high young lad pointing towards the preening majestic male lion, reflecting off of the majestic male lions 'licking' tongue.

There are only two folklore tales that ever show a character showing off their bright white teeth. One is of the ornery waist high young lad that's snickering at his big sister in the repetitive theme of when she and a beau are making out in the bushes at the springtime picnic. The other is of the taunting warrior braves unique facial expressions when he's making jeering gestures exposing his bright white teeth at the panting fair young maiden. He does it as he sits on his high horse and his jeering facial expression shows full rows of exposed clenched white teeth that make the warrior brave look like he's laughing mockingly at the fair young maiden. The hunter herder microlithic abstract artist's seldom show the Mammoth People with big smiles on their faces because most of the folklore tales involved miserable weary situations that they were cast in during the trials and tribulations that took place on their long epic journey to 'here'. If anything, you'll see dramatic facial expressions that are either of hollering and shouting faces or ones that express pure fear and horror.

The fourth version of the 'powwow' repetitive theme is of when grandma is shown riding in the sled that's being pulled by the lead mammoth, not atop the lead mammoth on her special armchair. The Mammoth People mammoth caravan was raided by the Palomino Pony People warrior braves and their galloping palomino horses. Grandma is shown hovering over her two toddler grandchildren who look like twins and are dressed in onesies or baby buntings. She's sitting on the front bench seat of the enclosed but topless mammoth pulled sled and she has her cape covered arms and her bonnet covered head down on the top of the front wall of the sled protecting her two toddler grandsons. She had shoved them down on their knees on the floor of the sled in front of her for protection the way that a mother duck would spread her wings over her defenseless ducklings to protect them from predators. Her toddler grandsons are shown either squatting down or on their knees on the floor of the sled between grandma's legs and below her chest and they definitely look like identical twins. The first one of this repetitive theme that I interpreted had an image of grandma with a spear through her chest while she hovered over and protected her toddler grandsons, simultaneously yelling at her fair young maiden granddaughter to run for her life to the sled and dive into it where she could hide behind the walls of it with her toddler twin brothers. Protective, but dying grandma's red blood was dripping down on one of the upward gazing toddlers' faces...and of course the flying submissive ewe spirit was gliding down to suck up her last exhaled breath or spirit to take it into the heavens to be with their deceased ancestors.

The fifth and final variation of the 'powwow' is an addition to the one of when irate grandma is riding atop the nervous lead mammoth sitting on her special armchair, and the mammoth caravan has been brought to a halt by her lead hunter herder son after the raid by the Palomino Pony People warrior braves and their galloping palomino horses. The gruff chief has dismounted from his palomino horse and is standing face to face with the lead hunter herder in front of the nervous lead mammoth while a crazy warrior brave chases the screaming fair young maiden toward them on his galloping palomino horse. However, in this version, irate grandma isn't just yelling at her two grandchildren about where they should stand, she's seen leaning over the right arm of her special armchair and yelling down between the right side of the nervous lead mammoth and the left side of the domestic milk cow, at mom herdswoman who's squatting down near the rear left side of the domestic milk cow. Frantic mom herdswoman has already removed her screaming hungry infant son's backboard carrier from the left shoulder of the domestic milk cow per irate grandma's shrieking instructions, and she has laid him backboard carrier and all on the ground next to her and is squirting fresh warm cow's milk all over his crying baby face in a lifesaving effort to get some into his constantly moving wide opened screaming mouth which is a desperate attempt to quiet him before the gruff chief or his crazy warrior braves become impatient and permanently silence all of them....

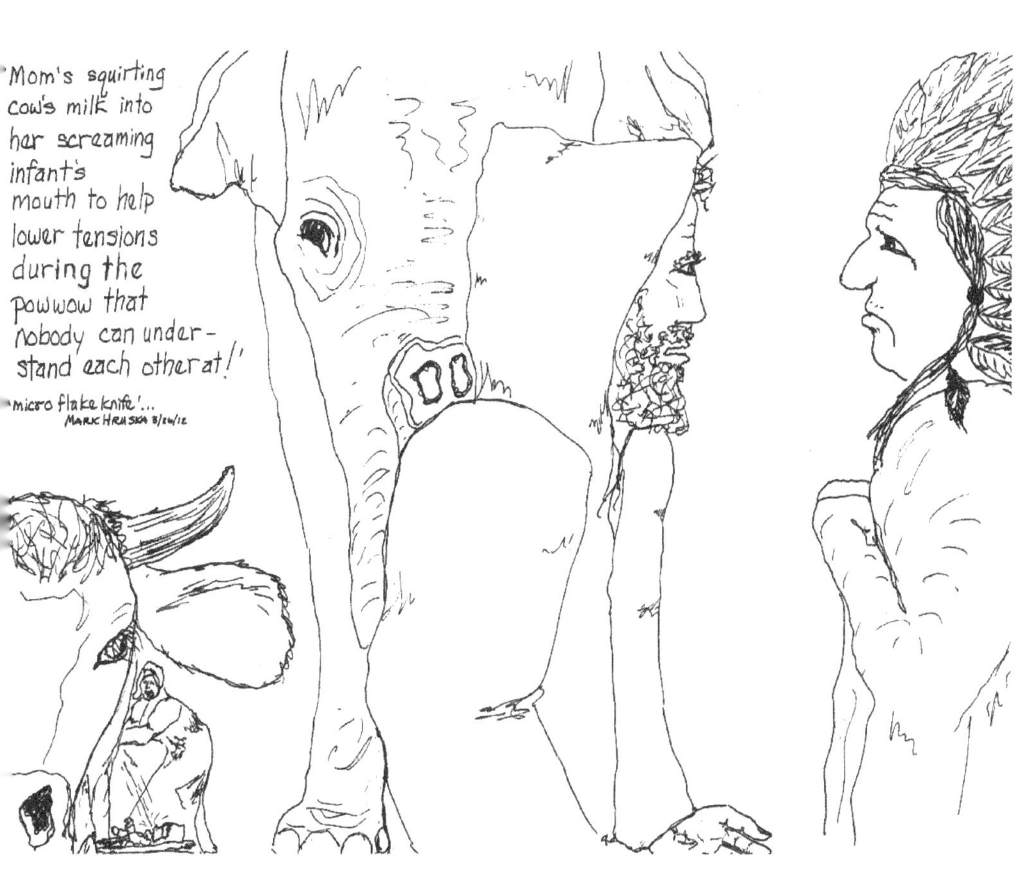

11. There's so much going on during the 'powwow' that even the nervous
lead mammoth needs reassurance as she continually sniffs over the lead
hunter herders shoulders towards his bearded face.

Chapter Ten

The Nuclear Mammoth People Family

The Pleistocene Caucasian nuclear family or as I call it, the Loving Mammoth People family that lived 'here' during the end of the Pleistocene era consisted of these main characters. I'll list them and then I'll mention what they're mostly known for in the Mammoth People hunter herder microlithic abstract artworks folklore tales....

Unlike the modern day nuclear family, the Paleo nuclear family definitely included grandma and grandpa. Other members include dad, mom, the teenage young lad, the teenage fair young maiden, the waist high young lad, the waist high young maiden the toddlers and the infant that's always shown wearing a onesie or baby bunting. Their domestic animals were considered family members too, especially the Scottie dog and the kitty because when they died the flying submissive ewe spirit glided down and sucked up their last exhaled breaths or their 'spirits' just like any other dying Mammoth People person, and carried them into the heavens to be with all of the deceased Mammoth People ancestors...and their pets. And, their pets were cremated just like the Mammoth People themselves were when they died, even though there may have only been their heads and a few other body parts to cremate after having been eaten by the big predators that attacked and killed them....and when I say 'them' I'm referring to either the humans or the pets. The complete domestic animal family members were the mammoth, the horse, the milk cow, the favorite ewe or ram, the Scottie and Bloodhound dogs and the kitty. Recently I've come to realize that the giraffe was also part of their domestic family...as unbelievable as that may sound. Nonfamily members that are supporting characters in the folklore tales are the sorceress and her three chanting assistants, the gruff chief, the crazy whooping and hollering warrior brave, the taunting warrior brave, the male lion and his lioness mate, the saber-toothed cat, the grizzly bear, the dire wolves and the rats. The Mammoth People hated rats.

Now, I'm going to go through the list and mention what the main characters of the Mammoth Peoples nuclear family are best known for starting with the most mentioned or should I say the most 'shown' member and that is 'grandma'. Unlike our modern times nuclear family that doesn't even mention grandma and grandpa, the Mammoth Peoples nuclear family didn't center on mom and dad, it centered on......

Grandma...she's by far the most visible image on the Mammoth People hunter herder microlithic abstract artwork's repetitive themes and is the very first Caucasian Mammoth People person that I saw when I first saw her riding on her special armchair atop the 'walking towards you' lead mammoth. I'm sure it's because of her wisdom, tenacity and the fact that she had a great deal to do with raising the grandchildren, teaching them the Mammoth People ways and traditions. She was definitely an important figure in the survival of all of our ancestors. She's seen as a loving kind shepherdess and as a strict sort of matriarch and usually has a bonnet on her head or with her capes hood or shawl over her bonnet. She is also shown as being crotchety or irate most of the time when shown during their trekking themed folklore tales.

Grandpa.....he's usually shown with a full white beard and mustache, is bald but has a hood or horse blanket draped over his bald head most of the time, and is feeble or sickly because you'll see him a lot when he's lying back at forty five degree angle on his travois when they were trekking. He's either shown ranting and in a delirious state of mind or pissed off and cursing depending on which folklore tale you are viewing. When he's standing or walking he's usually shown with a cane and in one popular folklore tale he's pissed off and cursing while he's shown hobbling towards the powwow with a windblown horse blanket draped over his injured bald head and over his shoulders. His cane comes in handy when he defends his waist high young lad grandson from a snarling dire wolf and there is one repetitive theme where he's shown as being disappointed in his teenage grandson because he couldn't stay on his bucking bull for a respectable amount of time. So he was very important in the growth and development of the teenage young lads because he made them tough like the hunter herders that they were going to have to be.

Dad hunter herder....is always shown as the 'lead' hunter herder so he's always serious and shown with a full dark bearded 'stern' looking face that always has 'handsome' features. Nevertheless, the hunter herder microlithic abstract artist's always make him look as handsome as they possibly can....because it's like doing your own portrait. Every hunter herder that I've seen on the microlithic abstract art was good looking or 'dashing'....how could that be? Perhaps it's because he or the younger version of himself is always the one that's creating the microlithic abstract artwork. He has that stern look on his handsome face because he's usually concentrating on the task at hand whether it be getting his family as far away from the violently erupting volcano that's chasing them out of their beloved homeland or holding down on the backs of grandmas legs while she tries to snag their fair young maiden out in the hole in the predator ice after she and the horse that she was riding plunged through it...while he firmly instructs mom to direct the nervous lead mammoth to kneel beside him and grandma. He will often be seen with his hands full, hanging on to a rein strap with his left hand while carrying his crotchety elderly mothers right stretcher pole that her special armchair is attached to, on his sore left shoulder. You'll often see him looking up or back over one of his shoulders like during the 'powwow' when he looks back up over one of them towards his shrieking irate overbearing elderly mother over the head of the nervous lead mammoth that's also fishing the end of her sniffing trunk over his shoulders for reassurance too. In other words, he bears a lot of responsibility on his shoulders

Mom herdswoman....is often seen with a worried looking face during all of the dramatic and epic events that take place on their long trek to 'here'. But, she's also shown as being composed and tries to maintain calmness, like her husband. Many of the repetitive themes show her caring for their infant who's usually dressed in an oncsie or baby bunting and who's usually strapped to a backboard and slung over the domestic milk cow's left shoulder. Mom walks between the domestic milk cow and the mammoth when they trek. That way she is almost 'face to face' with her infant. The front of his face is close to the right side of hers. Dad leads the mammoth by walking to the left and slightly ahead of her head. This way he and the infant can see each other too, not to mention that the mammoth's left eye can see dad and he can see her left eye when he looks back over his right shoulder. Grandma rides atop the mammoth on her special armchair where she has a 'bird's eye' view over their surroundings and can watch for lurking predators in the tall swaying prairie grass. She can easily converse with mom who's down to her right, dad who's to the front left of her, and the fair young maiden and grandpa who are to the left of her. She can even see how the infant is doing and he can see her when he looks up over mom's head. The fair young maiden is often shown riding the horse that's pulling grandpa's travois. The horse is walking abreast to the left of the mammoth just as the domestic milk cow is walking abreast to the right of the mammoth. Grandma and the fair young maiden can converse easily because they're both elevated and abreast of each other. The fair young maiden is slightly behind dad and out to his left.

One of mom herdswoman's most noticeable performances is in the popular folklore tale of when the fair young maiden and her horse fall through the predator ice. In it, mom herdswoman is shown confidently and firmly directing the nervous lead mammoth over to the edge of the hole in the predator ice where she is supposed to kneel down next to grandma and dad. This way concentrating grandma could hold onto one of her long tusks and then be able to reach further out into the hole with her extended shepherd's crook to try to snag the fair young maiden who's struggling to keep her chin above the icy cold sea water that's being churned up by her thrashing horse's flailing front feet and hooves.

Mom also seems to be the main character in one of the variations of the 'powwow' when she has to frantically try to quiet the hungry screaming infant by removing his carrier from the left shoulder of the domestic milk cow and lay him on the ground next to its left teats so that she could squirt fresh warm cow's milk into his constantly moving wide opened screaming mouth and silence him before the gruff chief and his warrior braves became more irritated than they already were.

The fair young maiden......is a vivacious and necessary nuclear family member especially since she has younger siblings that mom and dad need help with. She's been shown as a 'milk maiden' because the women are the ones that took care of the domesticated sheep and milk cows and they're the ones that milked the dehorned cows. The domesticated dehorned milk cow is often seen in the trekking scenes and she's carrying the infant who's strapped to a backboard, on her left shoulder (she's not always dehorned when seen trekking). This was a very useful situation because if the trekkers had to stop because of the screaming infant when they really didn't have time to stop because they were trying to get to a river or glacial ice meltwater stream before sunset, mom or grandma could quickly take the screaming infant off of the domestic milk cow's left shoulder. They could plop his carrier down on the ground near her udder while he was still strapped to it, and squirt fresh warm cow's milk in his screaming mouth to quiet him until they reached a river bank to make camp. The infant is always wearing a white onesie or baby bunting.

I seemed to have gotten sidetracked but now you know what the infant was best known for..... Another situation that shows how important the vivacious fair young maiden was is shown in the folklore tale of the 'epic deluge' when the strong swimming fair young maiden rescues her grandpa who was swept off of his travois and would have surely drowned. She gets him to the swimming mammoth and helps dad get him up on her back with the rest of the huddling lead family that included mom, the infant, the toddlers and the sobbing waist high young maiden who couldn't find her lost kitty. Sometimes they even hoisted the exhausted baby mammoth up there. The fair young maiden was also an overachiever and that is shown in one folklore tale that involves her riding her horse too far out ahead of her lead hunter herder dad to help him locate one of those big cats that irate grandma swore she saw lurking in the tall swaying prairie grass out ahead of the nervous lead mammoth. Because of her overconfidence she ends up being taken right off of her horse by the stalking saber-toothed cat right in front of her helpless dad which left a stunned expression on her silenced grandma's face.

The teenage young lad....is known for doing the things that will make him a strong hunter and herder like his dad. Things like bull riding which would come in handy when they broke horses. He's often seen hunting Canada geese from a camouflaged kayak but he's also shown sticking his nose where it doesn't belong because he's very interested in sex. One repetitive theme shows him watching mating lions from under a tree or under a rock ledge when what he didn't know was that another lioness from the pride was on the ledge above him or in the tree above him watching him. She ambushes him and when the mating lions finish what they were doing they eat him. That seems to be a very good lesson for oversexed inquisitive nosy teenage young lads who are shown with oversized nosy noses. He's also shown as being very compassionate or empathetic especially to his waist high young maiden little sister while at the same time being disgusted with his stern dad.

The waist high young lad....isn't much different than the bigger and older version of himself. He's usually shown as being rambunctious and ornery and he can range in age from toddler up to waist high. He wants to be like his lead hunter herder dad and walks next to the left side of him when they trek. Sometimes he gets too daring and gets out too far ahead in the tall swaying prairie grass and comes face to face with a stalking saber-toothed cat or a lurking lion. He's also shown as being mesmerized when he and dad are confronted and face to face with the gruff chief and his taunting warrior brave who's sitting atop his 'high horse' next to and slightly behind the gruff chief. He can't believe the gruff chief's ridiculous wardrobe nor can he believe what he's seeing when the taunting warrior brave makes jeering gestures at him and his frightened big sister who he just finished chasing over to the front of the mammoth and to her dad's side on his galloping palomino horse. The smaller or toddler waist high young lad is often shown as being rambunctious and gets himself into a lot of trouble when nobody is paying attention to him. In one repetitive theme he walks away from camp because he's enticed by the roaring glacial ice meltwater stream that he gets too close to and falls into only to be swept past his shocked female family members who are getting water for the evening meal. In another ornery performance that takes place at the 'summertime picnic' he's seen looking down from up in a tree that's on the riverbank and he has a smirk on his face. That's because he's covertly watching his big sister and her beau making out underneath the tree. The waist high young lad has also been known for coming face to face with those nasty dire wolves that attacked the summertime picnic but he's always fiercely defended by his loyal Scottie dog until grandpa or grandma get there and whack the snarling dire wolf over the head taking that snarl right off of its snout.

The waist high young maiden....is mostly seen in the most common of the repetitive themes that I call the 'volcanic mass exodus'. In this repetitive theme she goes from being mortified because her frightened kitty jumped on and scratched delirious grandpa's face, to being upset and sobbing. This is usually when she has to go 'march' out ahead of her compassionate teenage young lad front left porter big brother. She stops briefly in front of him to lay her head against his chest for sympathy and reassurance before continuing on to 'madly march' out ahead of him taking big marching steps while swinging her little cape covered arms wildly to and fro. That way crotchety grandma can keep a glaring eyeball on her and her naughty kitty that the madly marching waist high young maiden is scolding the way that crotchety grandma just scolded her. The waist high young maiden is almost always shown with her kitty and the waist high young lad usually will have the Scottie as a 'best bud'. One of the most heartbreaking folklore tales that I've interpreted involves the waist high young maiden falling through a lightly frozen over sea lion breathe hole when they were trekking across the predator ice. Mom should have been hanging onto her little hand better but she slipped through it so fast and just like that she was out of reach floating supine with her childlike face pressed up against the underside of the ice while dad, down on all fours peered helplessly at her from above the ice and grandma tried frantically to swipe her long shepherd's crook towards her with her upper body and head submerged in the sea lion breathe hole....only to watch the drowning waist high young maiden slowly sink into the dark icy cold abyss...

The Scottie...is grandma's protector and companion too, especially when she's out in the meadow watching over her domestic sheep and milk cows. The fierce little Scottie will fight to the death defending her if they're attacked by one of the many big predators. He can also be seen defending his waist high young lad during the summertime picnic when a pack of dire wolves attack. The fierce Scottie will get between his waist high young lad and the snarling dire wolf that are face to face with each other. He'll hold off the snarling dire wolf until grandpa or grandma can get to the scene of the incident and whack the snarling dire wolf over its snarling snout. Since he's a house dog he alerts his family members to the rats that may be chewing on the crying infants ears and I'm sure he occasionally catches the rats too.

The Bloodhound...is usually dad and grandpa's dog and he's with them when they herd their cattle and mammoth out on the open prairie. Not only was he a great watch dog, but he helped them round up and herd the domestic cattle and mammoth. The bloodhound pup is most often seen in the 'sorceress' folklore tale as a defender of unconscious grandpa because he lays his head across grandpas lower legs while keeping his sad eyes on the sorceress as she recites incantations and waves her cape covered arms that look like the Steller's sea eagle spirits black wings, over unconscious grandpa's face. Her flapping wings are wafting the smoke from the fireplace over grandpa's face until he miraculously chokes back to life.

The most important domestic animal was by far the lead mammoth. She plays an important role in the trekking themes and is central to the 'powwow' folklore tale, mainly because she was irate grandma's 'ride'. She is usually seen on the edge of the bigger flint artworks as a close-up image of the 'walking towards you' mammoth. But on the small flake knife ones, the clever way that the hunter herder microlithic abstract artist shows her in many of those storylines is to just show one of her appendages such as her wrinkly trunk or one of her ears like they do in the 'epic deluge' folklore tale. Since the only visible part of her swimming body's head is her raised trunk that's sticking up like a periscope and that she's breathing through, they could use it or one of her flapping ears as a close-up image that could have concentrating grandma's microlithic cognitive illusion reflection image reflecting off of them.

The black faced ram....was another domestic animal that was like a pet or family member because he and grandpa spent a lot of time together watching over the sheep in the meadow and they were like best buds. When they trekked, the ram always stayed near the side of grandpa and at times you could see that he was carrying water that was in opposing pottery jars that were hung over his shoulders. He most likely carried the drinking water.

The kitty plays a huge role in the Mammoth People microlithic abstract art because kitties meant so much to the toddler and waist high young maidens who were being told the folklore tales and they can readily relate to the characters in the tale when they involve kitties. He's the waist high young maiden's constant companion and you'll see him in many of the folklore tales, especially the 'volcanic mass exodus' where he instigates the conniption fit that crotchety grandma has in the first place. In the 'epic deluge' folklore tale, he's seen paddling for his life towards the rest of the rescued lead family who are riding atop the swimming mammoth's back behind grandma's special armchair. They're all calling out for 'Precious' especially his sobbing waist high young maiden.

We can't forget how important the domestic milk cow was and the central role that she played in some of the folklore tales especially the 'milking version' of the 'powwow'.

There are many other characters in the repetitive themes but it doesn't take long to figure out who the hunter herder microlithic abstract artists loved the most and who they loathed the most and were their greatest nemesis. They absolutely detested 'rats' and gave them red beady eyes because they couldn't keep them out of their homes that were built out of sod and that had thatch roofs. It's one of the main reasons that the waist high young maiden's kitty cats were so important to the nuclear family. The rats chewed on the Mammoth Peoples infant's ears.

The Mammoth People detested the whooping and hollering warrior braves more than the rats and to prove it they show them at times with red eyes like the rats. Their images are often on red stone because of their red skin and in one repetitive theme grandma is seen spitting on a dead one's war painted white face after his galloping horse lowered his head and put on the brakes and threw him while he was chasing the fair young maiden. She was carrying her kitty in one arm while she ran holding up her long dress skirt with the other free hand and her frightened kitty had hissed and clawed at the galloping palomino horses wide opened left eye that was right next to the right side of the running fair young maiden's right shoulder. This caused the horse to put on the brakes and the whooping and hollering warrior brave flew over his lowered head and bit the Pleistocene dust...after his neck tangled in the rein straps that ran out of slack, breaking it. Grandma spryly dismounted from the nervous lead mammoth to claim the dead warrior brave's fine palomino horse for her granddaughter to ride. While she was still bent over finishing untangling the rein straps from around the dead warrior brave's broken neck, she spit on his face which resulted in abhorred reactions by her fair young maiden granddaughter and the rest of the lead family who were standing off in the distance...next to the gruff chief.

The Mammoth People also loathed the saber-toothed cats, the lions, the short face and grizzly bears and the sneaky dire wolves...oh...and let's not forget about the bald eagle that swooped down and snatched up their little lambs.

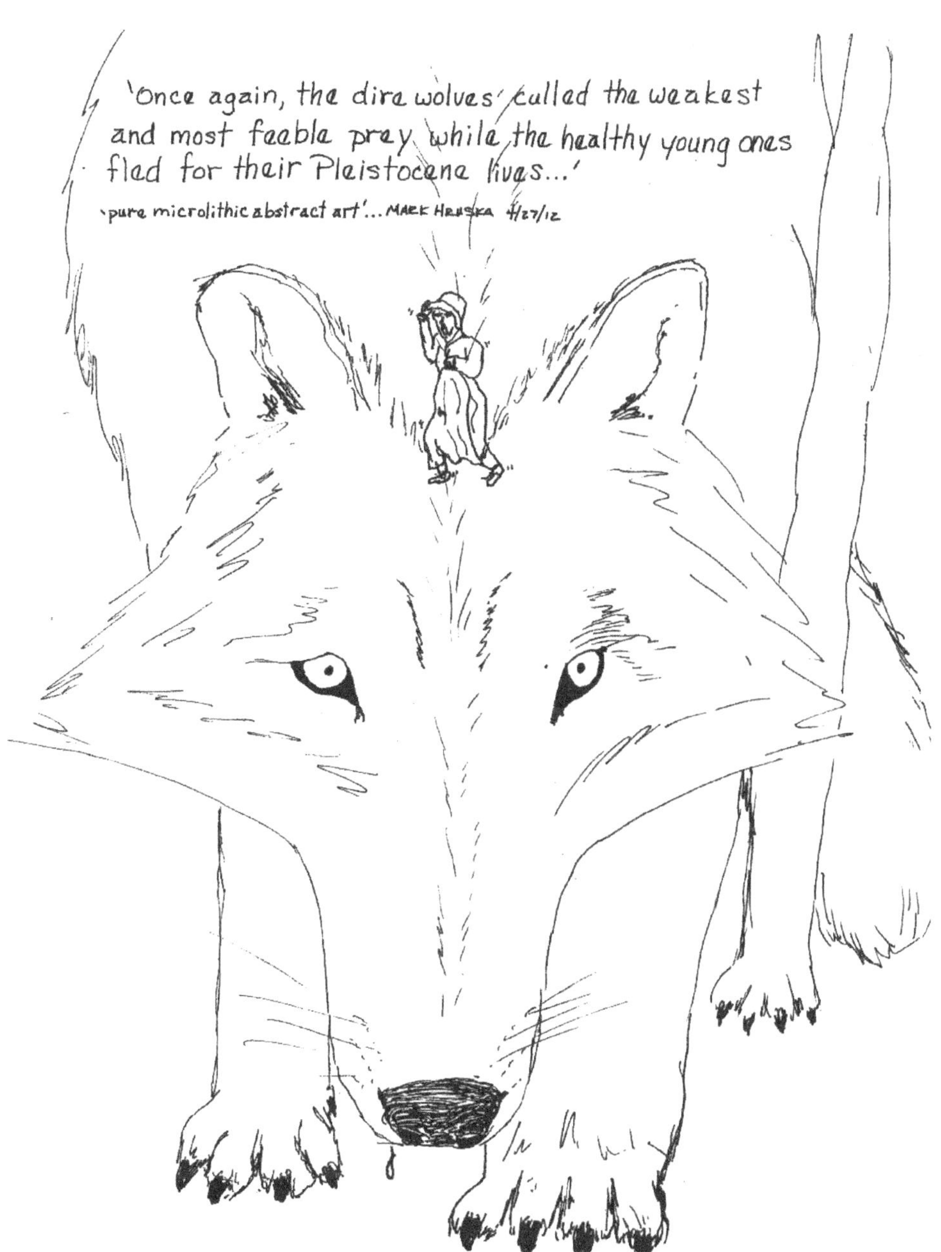

12. It's usually a pack or a pair of
dire wolves that attack the summertime picnic event.

Chapter Eleven

The Mammoth Peoples' Schools

In August of 2013 my neighbors to the east burned down a small farmstead house and had a bulldozer push the foundation in a hole and cover it up. This small square farmstead house was one half mile directly east of my home and it was no more than fifty feet from the river bank. The bulldozer that cleared away the foundation of the burnt up house also scraped off the cement sidewalks and pushed them over the river bank that is just a few feet east of where they had laid for the better part of a century.

The week after they cleared the sidewalks off we received about one-half inch of rain so when I went on my two mile run that I usually take past the place several times a week, I thought I'd stop and see if I could find any artifacts in the soft black dirt on the top of that high river bank where the sidewalks were scraped away. There remains a good sized ice cave that the homesteaders put chunks of frozen river ice for their wooden icebox refrigerators, to the southeast of where that side walk was. The neighbors had given me permission to look for artifacts on any of their ground that was around the river so that wasn't a problem. One quarter of a mile further east on the east side of the river is my '3b' herd stead site and I've always wondered if there could be artifacts on the high spot on the west side of the river next to the road where our homesteader ancestors would have naturally put a house like so many of my other sites.

When I searched the site I was disappointed because I didn't find any flint or pottery shard artifacts but I did find small pieces of heat treated soft siltstone that was like limestone but different shades of red, pink, orange, grey and white. They were unlike anything that I had ever seen and were concentrated in one area as if they were in several small piles in that small area before the cement sidewalk was poured over them. Then the tops of the piles were slightly spread out when the bulldozer took the tops off of them and smeared them in the direction that it was pushing the sections of cement sidewalk towards the river bank that they were pushed over. I also found several pieces of heat treated siltstone nodules that looked like something in between flint and the soft siltstone mediums that the small pieces were made of. They were blood red and grey colored and about two to three inches in diameter...and polished. I had never seen stone like this on any of the other herd stead sites nor had I ever seen it in my entire farming career. After cleaning up just a few of those first pieces I realized instantly that I was on to a cache of some sort because of the concentration of all of the small pieces of siltstones that had originally come from the larger cobble sized polished pieces. They all looked black or dark grey until I washed and brushed them clean with a toothbrush.

Over the course of the next week, I ran down there several times and with a long narrow screwdriver I sliced through the soft black soil to a depth of no more than six inches until it pinged against the siltstone. I found five distinct small piles of these kinds of heat treated siltstone as if they had been on top of a table at one time. That first pile that I found even had a piece of preserved wood under it, if that could at all be possible. It's as if the five small piles were on a four by eight foot wooden table. When I realized this I could instantly envision a sod schoolhouse around the table right there on that high west bank of the river and that this was in fact the site of a sod schoolhouse. I also realized that the tiny pieces of thin flat soft siltstone were colors that resembled the pinkish shades of color that would imitate the Caucasian Mammoth Peoples skin colors with the redder shades imitating the Palomino Pony People warrior braves and the gruff chief's skin colors. As I mentioned earlier, these pieces aren't found on any of the other herd stead sites and the amount and concentration of it clearly hinted at a cache of some kind. It wasn't until I cleaned the stone that I instantly saw all of the microlithic abstract art or attempted art that was on it. This was indeed the remnants of a sod schoolhouse.

The small piles of tiny flat narrow pieces were definitely situated around a wooden table where the students who ranged in age from beginner to more advanced, worked on their lessons. The headmaster of this '3d' school site, created and used the biggest pieces of rubbed out polished grey and red siltstone as teaching tools much as a teacher would use a book to teach today. These pieces aren't found on any of the other herd stead sites because all of the pieces stayed 'in' the sod schoolhouse. The beginner student would attempt to create optical illusion close-up images of the Mammoth Peoples two main repetitive themes which were of the 'volcanic mass exodus' and the 'powwow', on the biggest pieces. Any of the reduction pieces that they made but were of poor quality art were then used by more advanced students to do the same thing until you got down to the smallest pieces that the most advanced students then worked to create a complete microlithic abstract artwork that had a complete repetitive theme on it that included the combined optical and cognitive illusion close-up images with the microlithic cognitive or combined optical and cognitive illusion reflection images reflecting off of it. Only then could they graduate and go onto one of the other Mammoth People schools that were of higher learning such as the potsherd one located on the hill at the '2a' site where I found so many of the bigger pieces of pottery shards that included part of the rim of the pot and that were made into fantastic microlithic abstract artworks. Most of them were concentrated on a certain area of the hill as if they came from a single cache pit that may have been in one of the houses, or so I used to think.

Now I believe that they were in the schoolhouse that had bench seats and that was also the religion and town hall building where they held meetings to decide how to amongst other important things, go about finding and killing the rogue lions that were killing and eating their domestic animals....or their family members. The potsherds are 'microlithic' abstract artworks too even though they are made mostly of baked clay, because the hunter herder microlithic abstract artist used the tiny pieces of sand aggregate that are embedded in the fractured edges of the baked clay, as the heads and faces of the repetitive themes characters or as the microlithic reflection images that were reflecting off of the main characters heads and faces that 'arc' the whole potsherd.

I'll explain it like this... There are at least three criteria that when combined will tell you if you're viewing a Mammoth Peoples potsherd microlithic abstract artwork. First of all, the edges of the potsherd will be slightly rubbed off all the way around its perimeter on both sides of it...and no that won't just make it look like a rubbing tool. The second way to tell is by taking a close look at the edges that are sandwiched between the lighter yellowish clay colored outer side of the shard and the darker or greyish inner side of it. If you see that most of the sand aggregate has been removed leaving only a few choice pieces, especially white, pink, red or translucent pieces, then there's a really good chance that they are individually rubbed and etched out microlithic statuesque artworks of the heads and faces of the characters that are an integral part of the theme of the piece, the red colored ones would be naturally reserved for the gruff chief or the warrior brave's characters...sometimes irate grandma's beet red face. The third and most telling way to know if you're viewing a pottery shard Mammoth People hunter herder abstract artist abstract artwork is if you see very fine swirly parallel lines on the edge of the potsherd between the inner and outer surfaces. How the hunter herder microlithic abstract artist created these incredibly fine swirly etched out marks is a mystery, but the best that I can figure is that they continually rubbed in a slow and deliberate steady motion with an incredibly hard and honed pointy sharp splinter of bone, possibly a bone awl that was shaped like a modern day pencil. I'm convinced that they used the same methods to rub out the imagery that is seen on the flint microlithic abstract artworks as well as that seen on the siltstone and limestone microlithic abstract artworks. The students at this school also learned how to create rubbed and etched out 'snapshot' scenes on the pottery shards, usually on the light grey slip that's on the inside side of the potsherds.

Another one of the more advanced schools is located at the '5a' school site. Nowhere else have I found such an incredible amount of small flint flake knives that are the size of the struck off or knapped off flint flakes that would be produced when the hunter herder created his spear points and large oval knives by percussion strikes or by knapping. These supposed waste flakes are normally referred to as debitage. When I first found the site, I thought that it had to have been a place that the historic Indians were making their spear and arrow points......but you found very view of them or failed attempts at making them. It just couldn't be this kind of flint debitage because it was as if it was cached in this one place from all of the surrounding herd stead sites....not created on site. Many of them have 'erailure' marks and 'bulbs of percussion' on them with conchoidal marks which show that they were struck off of a core or a larger knife or spear point.

These seemingly useless heat treated flint flakes were created by being knapped off or struck off of one of the herd steads hunter herder's spear points or oval knives that he was creating at home. It was collected and saved as were all of the knapped or struck off pieces of different kinds of heat treated flint at all of the surrounding herd steads. The debitage was then brought to the school by the student to be used for their lesson plans which were to rub and etch out microlithic abstract artworks in their microlithic abstract art figurative language while incorporating images and scenes from their most popular repetitive themes or folklore tales. This is how the students learned to work so intimately with stone which their lives depended on and in doing so it also sharpened their visual, their cognitive and their dexterity skills as they worked to bring out impossibly small imagery as reflections that were reflecting off of rubbed and etched out closer up statuesque imagery, and then incorporate it into scenes that you could advance to by turning or rotating the piece while telling the folklore tale...as if you were turning the pages of a modern day two dimensional storybook.

The headmaster of the school undoubtedly created the most fantastic microlithic 'master' abstract artworks that he then used to teach his students with so that they could attempt to imitate them. Nothing went to waist, virtually every one of the heat treated spent flint flakes that was brought to the school was fashioned into a microlithic abstract artwork, some being just of individual heads or faces of the characters of the folklore tales while others that were created by the more advanced students, incorporated microlithic reflection imagery that was reflecting off of those characters heads and faces. All of these pieces were concentrated in about a fifty by thirty foot area on the fairly steep sloping east bank of the river. It became crystal clear to me that the Mammoth People children were bringing this vast array of different heat treated flint flakes to their school to be used as the medium to learn the microlithic abstract arts figurative language on. Remember, the goal was to make the smallest pieces with the most complete repetitive themes or folklore tales on them.....that's what distinguished the superior student from the average one. And that's why I didn't find the Caucasian Mammoth People until after I found the birds and the Pleistocene animals of their time because the people's heads and faces tend to be on these tiniest pieces which makes them look the most realistic, not to mention that the individual round and oval fossils that are embedded in the heat treated fossiliferous flint...look just like Caucasian people's heads and faces, especially if you wanted to create a microlithic cognitive illusion reflection scene of the multitudes of miserable weary Mammoth People trekkers that you see in their most popular folklore tales.

Some of those microlithic cognitive illusion images that are created by the tiny round and oval shaped fossil heads and fossil faces that have distinct eyes and mouths, look virtually indistinguishable from our more modern day 'impressionists' oil paintings by the Masters such as I've seen on the Britain Master oil painter Joseph Turner's pieces that are called 'Light and color' and 'Shade and Darkness'. They could be called 'expressionist' oil paintings too, but when I first saw them I instantly thought that the small brilliantly illuminated heads and faces of the people that had pinpoint eyes and mouths on the 'Light and Color' one, were the nearest thing that I can think of that demonstrates the look and feel of the Mammoth People microlithic abstract art's microlithic cognitive illusion imagery of the multitudes of miserable weary trekkers who's heads and faces are being illuminated by the glow of the violently erupting volcano or being illuminated by the flashes of lightning from its broiling ash cloud that's pursuing them in the 'volcanic mass exodus' folklore tale. The 'Shade and Darkness' one also gives the look and feel that the 'volcanic mass exodus' folklore tale does, taking place in the middle of the Pleistocene night, because of the way that you see the right side view of one horse with its head turning to its right side, and the front right side view of another horse's head barely visible through the dark with dark clouds of dust engulfing them. That right side view of that first horse is what the 'beast of burden' horse that's pulling delirious grandpa's travois looks like when he tries to get his head either over or under the left or right travois pole so that he can try to see what's going on behind him alongside of delirious grandpa's travois while the roaring broiling volcanic ash cloud engulfs...or pounces on them. Seeing how both oil paintings are the same size and have that oval swirl appearance around their perimeters, I would say to view both of them side by side and then imagine in your 'mind's eye' that they were the same scene only you are seeing them during two separate flashes of lightning. You would get the feel for how the sobbing waist high young maiden and her compassionate big brother and the rest of their dysfunctional lead family felt when they were held up in the middle of the narrow windy mountain pass with the multitudes of miserable weary Mammoth People trekkers coming down the pass and splitting to either side of them as they hobbled on past them...

The most incredible discovery that I made actually searching for a possible school site took place at the '3d' sod schoolhouse site where the headmaster and his students specialized in the heat treated siltstone medium to create their microlithic abstract art. It had virtually no potsherds or small flint flakes or any other kind of artifacts that you would associate with a dwelling or herd stead site so they were only working on these particular soft heat treated siltstones and some bones. If an excited student inadvertently brought a piece of the siltstone art home to show mom or dad what he accomplished at school that day, the Mammoth People parents would recognize the stones immediately and make sure that they sent them back to school with the student the next day because older more experienced students would take the larger reduced pieces of the soft siltstone to make smaller and smaller more complex microlithic abstract artworks.....after praising their gifted child for the fine work that he created of course.

It's easy to see the different skill levels of the children starting with the very large pieces down to the complex combined optical and cognitive illusion close-up images that have the microlithic reflection images reflecting off of them. The very large pieces that the headmaster made as teaching tools, exactly replicate a microlithic abstract artwork that would be on a heat treated flint piece except that it's much larger. This helps the beginner students understand exactly what the teacher wants them to do before they take their skills to the microlithic level. The large pieces were created by the headmaster himself and they were meant to be an all-inclusive teaching tool much like the Webster dictionary was for me when I attended my one room country schoolhouse. Today I live exactly half way between the two schoolhouse sites which locate my residence one half mile from both of them and both of them are within sight of my home. The '3d' sod schoolhouse site that taught its students how to create microlithic abstract art in three dimensions (which has nothing to do with why it was labeled 3d) on heat treated siltstone, is located one half mile directly east of my home on the west bank of the river, while the one room country schoolhouse where I learned to read and write in two dimensions was one half mile directly west of my home.

This heat treated siltstone cache proves that the Mammoth People children had a structured life that included going to school, most likely during the summer months, and learning to 'think' in a figurative manner instead of the way we were taught which was a literal one. Instead of going up to the chalkboard in front of the entire one room classroom and perform structured grammar sentences or doing a math equation, they would be told to take a specific color of soft siltstone and create certain scenes from their 'volcanic mass exodus' or from their 'powwow' folklore tales. There were more than twenty of these repetitive themes or folklore tales but these two are the most popular and all of the themes were meant to teach the Mammoth People children about the trials and tribulations of their ancestors and the sacrifices that they made to get to 'here'. The flying submissive ewe spirit was included in all of them of course because that was their religious belief. More advanced students would be instructed to not only produce those repetitive themes scenes but to create them as microlithic reflections off of one of the main character's heads or faces possibly off of the underside of one of the flying submissive ewe spirits extended wings as she glided down to suck up the dying Mammoth People's last exhaled breaths which was their spirits, and take them up into the heavens to be with their deceased ancestors. This required intense physical dexterity and advanced cognitive concentration to be able to plan several moves in advance in a game of Paleo chess knowing what the outcome will be before making a single move, otherwise you ruin the whole piece that you were trying to rub out a specific microlithic image out of that was embedded in the stone and that was going to be the center of the swiping paw of the 'predators bent foreleg featuring the prey that it's stalking' art form that you were creating. I can just hear the school's headmaster all of those millennia ago trying to motivate one of the 'slower' students to try harder and do a better job of rubbing and etching out the lesson that was being taught that day.

Among the vast amount of heat treated siltstone microlithic abstract artworks that I found at the '3d, school site' I also found gravel head microlithic abstract art pieces and worked bone micro artworks. Many of them were also created by the headmaster of the sod schoolhouse to be emulated too. What you didn't find were pieces done on flint, stone or potsherds like I find at all of the herd stead sites. Everything that was done at the sod schoolhouse, stayed at the sod schoolhouse just as everything from home stayed at home. I think I found only two tiny potsherd pieces and only three or four flint pieces that were obviously brought unintentionally by students. And I have never found anything that remotely resembles the easily identifiable heat treated siltstone on any of the herd stead sites....ever.....which makes it all the more unbelievable that I found the heat treated siltstone to begin with, mind you, it was all covered with soil and looked almost black. I really only noticed it because of the unusual shapes of the pieces that I found first, and I didn't know that it was reddish, Caucasian flesh colored, purple, yellowish and cream colored until I thoroughly washed it off.

I always had it in the back of my mind that that high spot on the west bank of the river would have been a good place to have a Mammoth People sod house that would have a thatch gabbled roof which is why someone in recent times 'did' build a house there. All of the pieces of heat treated siltstone were concentrated in five or six piles around what I believe to have been a large wooden table. Everything, including the sod schoolhouse that had a thatched gabled roof, simply deteriorated and collapsed around the piles which for the most part remained undisturbed until the bulldozer that cleared the cement sidewalk that was directly above them spread out the top parts of the piles of heat treated siltstone which enabled me to see the unusual stone among the other debris of the demolished house in the first place. I had noticed that the pieces didn't resemble the busted up cement, brick and cement block that was scattered all around. And why were there so many tiny little pieces that could only have been created by hand? What could have broken them up so fine and yet kept them in a concentrated place.

It didn't take long to figure it all out after I took some of the pieces home and washed them off...I remind you that all of this was done on my normal two mile run that took me no more than sixty feet from the gravel road to the site. Once I cleaned the small pieces off, I immediately saw my Mammoth People microlithic abstract arts figurative language and their repetitive themes. As with all of the herd stead sites, I realized that there was no way that the Mammoth People simply walked away from all of this microlithic abstract artwork that taught their children how to make it in the first place...and that most likely is the very school that had taught the surrounding hunter herders how to make the pieces that I deciphered the microlithic abstract artwork from and that eventually led me to the sod schoolhouse site. That's right. I figured out their microlithic abstract arts figurative language from the microlithic abstract artworks that the grownup hunter herders created, and that knowledge enabled me to see the microlithic abstract art on the heat treated siltstone that taught them how to make it in the first place, bringing everything full circle. Obviously, not all of the art was created by the adults who had gone to that sod schoolhouse but depending on how long they occupied this area, a great deal of it may have been. At any rate, the genius headmaster of the sod schoolhouse had some part in teaching me which ultimately enlightened us of their very existence.

I can honestly give credit to every headmaster of all of the schools that I found, in playing a pivotal role in identifying themselves in prehistory simply because of their microlithic abstract 'masterpiece' artworks that I interpreted and that made it easier for me to decipher and then read their microlithic abstract art figurative language.

The siltstone microlithic abstract art that was left in situe at the '3d' school site demonstrates that the Mammoth People herd stead families had to have been raided by the Palomino Pony People warrior braves. They either had to leave in a big hurry or were murdered on the spot because they didn't have time to collect their most valuable belongings and flee just as their ancestors did when the violently erupting volcano chased them out of their beloved homeland in the middle of the Pleistocene night. There are no microlithic abstract artworks found that reveal what happened next except for a few found at the '1c' 'community site' or village site where I believe the Mammoth People made their last stand. On that site I found some very convincing pieces that showed the warrior braves attacking the hunter herders two to one with their war clubs that they swung as they attacked on their 'running like the wind' or galloping palomino horses. Let me remind you that the Mammoth People hunter herders created 'all' of the microlithic abstract art, so everything that I learned about both cultures is being seen through the eyes of the bias Mammoth People hunter herders and of course, the headmaster and his students who mysteriously and suddenly abandoned their sod schoolhouse. They left their piles of heat treated siltstone artworks or their lesson plans right on top of the work table as if they put them away after class and intended to get them out the next day. That day never came....and the artworks were rediscovered thirteen millennia later by someone who only could have found them after he figured out their microlithic abstract art figurative language that was taught to him by the heat treated flint artifacts discovered at their herd stead sites, that they were taught to make at the school that they went to when they grew up...mind blowing, but true....

One of the other incredibly important Mammoth People school sites that I found is at the '4c, school site'. The reason that it's so significant is that the headmaster of this school concentrated on teaching his students not on heat treated siltstone, but on limestone. The soft limestone was easy to rub and etch out imagery on much like the siltstone at the '3d, school site', but without the colorful pinkish purple and grey hues...just white, which when you think about it, represented how you'd see everything during the bright flashes of lightning in their most popular folklore tale of the 'volcanic mass exodus'. They rubbed and etched out the lightning illuminated imagery with their sharp pencil shaped bone awls that were most likely honed to a point by....limestone. I have some of these bone awls that I found with the heat treated siltstone at the '3d school' site and they were most likely honed to a fine point tip on the very siltstone that they were using as a medium to etch.

I also figured out that the reason that it's easiest to view the interpretations of the rotational change-up microlithic abstract artworks while you hold them with your left hands fingers is because most of the Mammoth People hunter herder microlithic abstract artists were naturally right handed, holding the pointy bone awl rubbing tool with their right hands fingers like a pencil while holding the artwork that they were creating, with their left hands fingers. This is also why it's natural for me to hold the piece with my left hands fingers while my right one can write and record while I interpret it... I'm simply replacing their bone awl with my pen or pencil.

The summer of 2014 yielded an incredible amount of artifacts from all of the sites because of the heavy rains we had in August, many of which were three inch gully washers. I spent quite some time walking up and down washed out rows in hot cornfields to pick up enough artifacts to keep me busy cleaning, cataloging and interpreting all winter. Before that season began I thought that I had come full circle and had learned just about all I was going to learn about the Mammoth People and their nemesis the Palomino Pony People, but was I ever wrong.

The biggest discovery that summer was about just how much the Mammoth People worked with limestone. I've been finding limestone abstract art on just about all of the sites and knew what I was seeing especially on the '2d' site. But once I really focused on it after all of the rains that summer, I found that limestone was the medium that was used in a big way to teach the Mammoth People children how to create the microlithic abstract art by starting big and taking it down to the microlithic level as they got better at their craft.

I've also known for some time now that they used limestone as a rubbing agent on flint to rub down to the cognitive illusions that they saw in the flint, sort of like sandpaper. I found a new site on the south side of the river on 21-13-2e that was like another school site....a limestone medium school site. Then I found a few fantastic small pieces along with flint on my David City farm, quite by accident I might add. Needless to say, the rest of the summer, I kept my eyes opened for any limestone lying around in the fields, especially hand held size pieces.

Up to now I thought that nearly all of the limestone that I was seeing out in the fields and especially on the abandoned farmed over farmstead sites was from limestone that was used for foundations of farm buildings and that it had just broken up after years of farm implements hitting it and reducing it. The site that I found the most limestone on over the years and that I concentrated on this last summer was at '4c' because I knew that an old corn crib stood over and protected that site and kept it from being tilled for most of the one hundred fifty years that folks farmed here. New owners bought the farm in 2015 and they deep disked the site which brought up many incredible artifacts that were of course interred with all of the other debris of the homesteader farm yard like many of the Mammoth People herd stead sites that I've located over my lifetime. Finding and picking up the newly brought up and exposed artifacts right away avoided serious farm implement damage (with permission of course).

I also carried some of the big pieces of limestone to the pickup just on a hunch not really expecting them to be anything more than busted up limestone from the more recent homestead yards house or barn. I knew that it was coming up from a deeper stratum that shouldn't have the more recent limestone in it and it was intermixed with outstanding Paleo artifacts like a beautiful hand ax which happened to be identical in shape to one of the symmetrical pieces of limestone that had smoothed off knife edges. You could also tell that it was a different kind of limestone than the limestone that was used for the foundations of the more recent homestead yards houses and outbuildings. It all laid on and under my bench in the garage in plastic Walmart sacks until the fall when I finally had time to get to it. I 'gently' cleaned it up with water and a soft toothbrush, which you have to do because the outer layer will just slough away from all of the millennia of laying buried in the dirt or from being weathered if it had been exposed to the elements. Some of the well preserved pieces were etched and rubbed out as if they were soft chalk and that's how the children learned to work with stone.

The largest piece of Mammoth People hunter herder microlithic abstract art, other than the red granite gruff chief's head that I have in my basement research room, is now a limestone abstract artwork that has the complete repetitive theme of the 'sorceress' conducting an exorcism on unconscious grandpa in the rat infested cottage. The rats choke and cough just like grandpa when he's miraculously brought back to life as the sorceress wafts smoke from the fireplace over his face that ends up collecting in the ceiling rafters of the cottage's gabled roof. The rats are on top of the wooden ceiling rafters above the ceremony and the waist high young maiden sees them because her kitty that she's always holding crawls up her right shoulder to get closer to them. The huge piece of limestone that I set in the back of my pickup and cleaned up several months later 'is' the combined optical and cognitive illusion extremely close-up image of the front left side view of one of those coughing rat's heads and you are seeing him that big or close up through the eyes of the sorceress. She's seeing him so up close to her face because she's peering skyward or heavenward, which is upward towards the smoke filled gabled roof of the cottage and its wooden ceiling rafters that the choking rats were clinging to while she recited incantations. The choking rats close-up head is an 'opposing head' to the close-up image of the sorceress's head and face that's reciting incantations to the Steller's sea eagle spirit while she flaps her black cape covered arms and wafts smoke over unconscious grandpa's face. You see the rat's face the way that she sees him peering over the edge of the wooden ceiling rafter as she looks up towards the smoke filled ceiling and beckons to the Steller's sea eagle spirit to take away the spell that the vipers that bit grandpa when he laid down to take a nap on his walk with his bloodhound pup, put on him. And the rat sees the sorceress's loudly talking face that's reciting incantations, the way that you see her on the other side of the limestone opposite the rats head and face. What's so amazing about the nearly perfect and undamaged large piece of limestone abstract art is that it's the shape of a huge prismatic knife. It was a perfect storytelling tool and it is created in the exact way that all of the microlithic repetitive themes are on flint prismatic knives. It's as if you simply took everything that's on that limestone piece and shrunk it down to the microlithic level that the advanced students would be working to create.

And speaking of those working students, I have found the equivalent of several five gallon buckets full of hundreds of rubbed down cobble sized and smaller limestone pieces that are from palm size to as small as you can get with three adjacent sides that would be where the ends of one hands thumb, index and middle fingers pinched together, all adjacent to the flat rubbing side of the piece. Many of these cobblestone sized pieces were actually works of microlithic abstract art with rubbed and etched out head's and faces on them.

During the fall of 2014 I cleaned, cataloged and interpreted more pieces of limestone abstract art that I found on my home place that I've farmed and lived on most of my life. I know now that the hillside site that is situated on one of the rolling hills that run parallel and to the northwest of the river valley that has so many of my other herd stead sites that the Mammoth People lived on, was a school site that taught the young hunter herders the craft of the microlithic abstract art while they watched over their grazing cattle, sheep and mammoth. There are no other artifacts at this site which is about the circumference of a large building, which is why I never paid any attention to it because a small farm yard had been there up until the nineteen forties or early fifties. If I didn't know the Mammoth Peoples microlithic abstract art figurative language I would never have understood what went on at that spot over thirteen millennia ago. You can clearly see that the palm size pieces of limestone were worked into specific shapes with the Mammoth Peoples repetitive themes incorporated on them with the appropriate microlithic reflection imagery and you could also see the damage that modern day farm machinery inflicted on them. Either way, the artifacts couldn't have been created by simply having been chipped off of larger limestone blocks that were foundation stones from homestead farm buildings and then reduced by being repeatedly hit by farm implements over seventy or eighty years of being farmed over.

I found another school site on the south side of the river on another farm that I farmed my whole farming career. Some of the limestone microlithic abstract artworks that I've found there have some fantastic art on them.

That's at least six possible school sites and the first thing that you'll say is if it were true, why would only twenty some herd stead sites have that many schools? Well....for one thing, they very likely didn't exist at the same time and if the Mammoth People occupied this area for more than a hundred years you could see where it was possible. But I really do think that they had several schools at the same time and here's why. The school on the hill at the '2a' site seemed to focus on teaching its students how to incorporate the microlithic abstract art on potsherds, especially potsherd rim pieces. The school at the '4c' site focused on teaching the beginner students how to create microlithic abstract art along with all of its rules and art forms on big pieces of limestone and then take it down to more of a micro level.

The brilliant headmaster at the '3d' school site exclusively used heat treated siltstone, none of which was bigger than the palm of your hand, for the easiest to read and interpret teaching pieces, but much smaller for the pieces that he was trying to get his more advanced students to replicate or emulate. Then, the headmaster at the '5a' school site had the most difficult job of teaching his students how to work heat treated flint debitage into microlithic abstract artworks and incorporate images and scenes of the Mammoth People's folklore tales into the tiniest of those flint flakes and still try to make them function as a utilitarian eating utensil with a scraper edge and a honed or knapped knife edge on it and perhaps even make it into a 'backed' knife....or a seam ripper....or a shaft scraper. Many supposedly 'shaft' scrapers are simply crescent shaped rubs on the edge of the piece that were crafted exactly like you see them in an attempt to orient the 'rotational change-up' microlithic abstract artwork so that the interpreter of the folklore tale was holding it in the upright position. The size of the crescent shaped rub could even determine if the child's index finger or thumb would fit into it helping them positon the piece to see the next image or scene. The more I learned from these Mammoth People school sites, the more I realized how structured the children's lives really were, which was no different than mine was when I went to my one room country schoolhouse....after all, they still had the same amount of hours in a day that I had and school kept my rambunctious self out of my parent's hair while they did all of the work that they had to do to survive...just like the Mammoth People did.

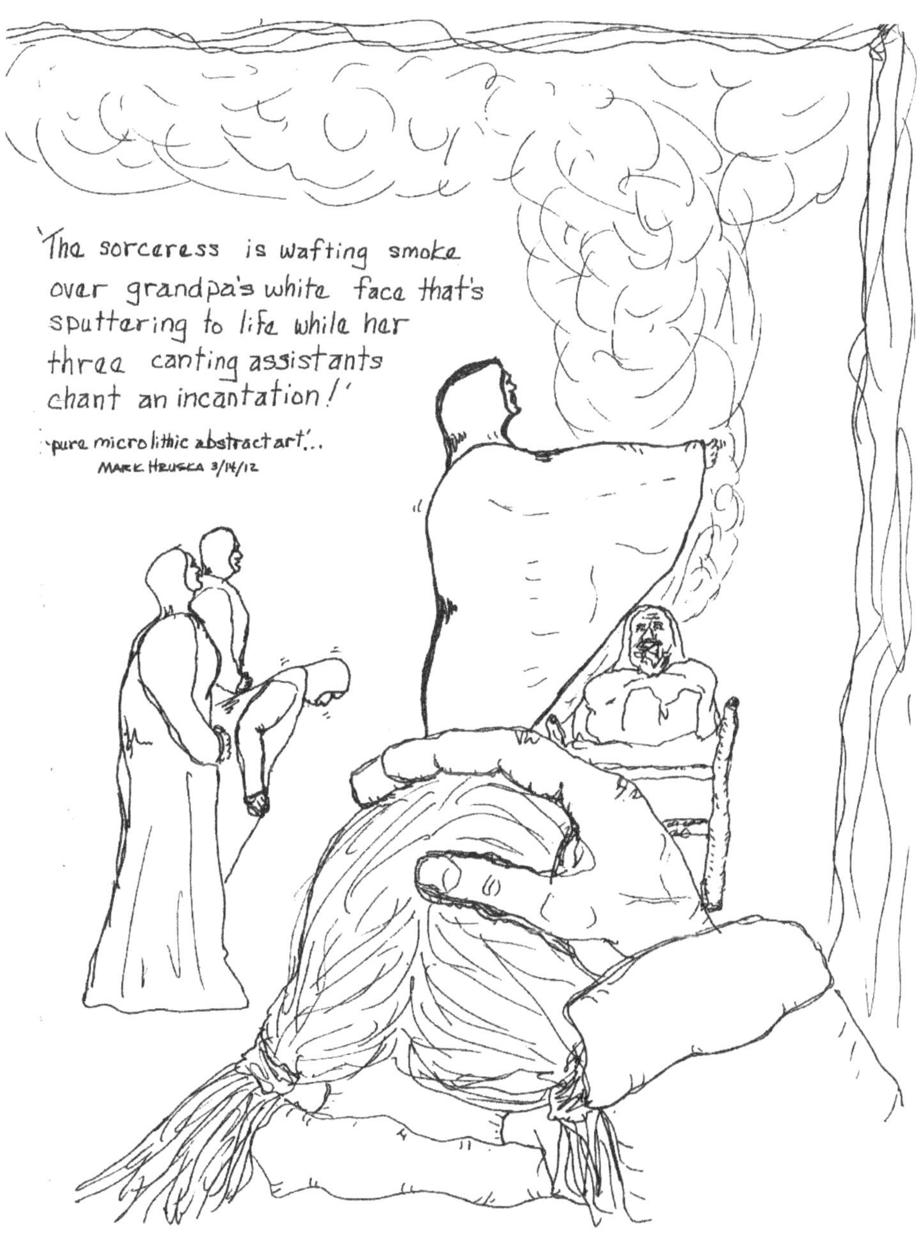

13. Concerned grandma is standing in the open doorway of the cottage holding her granddaughter in front of her while the sorceress and her three chanting assistants preform the exorcism ceremony on unconscious grandpa.

Chapter Twelve

What it Took to Find
All of That Stuff

In 2015 I cleaned the equivalent of four full 'five gallon' buckets of heat treated stone that I had gathered from the '1c' site when I was a kid in my early teens. I had carried all of that supposed debris off the field in readily available plastic 'Wonder Bread' sacks (readily available because my family that consisted of thirteen children...ate a lot of Wonder Bread from the day old bread store in Columbus, Nebraska) and I dumped it on a pile on the river bank next to where there was a cement bridge that later washed out from frequent flooding. The flooding also buried the pile with at least six inches of soil that later grew over with trees and weeds.

About four years before I had figured out the Mammoth People's microlithic abstract arts figurative language I realized that it was on everything that they used, so I went back and found the pile by probing for it with a long pointy steel rod. It took some searching but I eventually found it when the rod 'pinged' on top of the flattened out pile of rock that I had made there nearly forty years earlier. I excavated the pile and tried to get every single artifact that I had placed there. The remarkable thing about this story is the fact that had I not inadvertently picked up all of the rocks so that I wouldn't have to pick them up again when I went looking for 'arrowheads', I wouldn't have saved them from the inevitable damage that would have been done to them from forty years of farm machinery driving over, slicing and dicing them and because of it they're some of the most pristine pieces that I have found.

As I was going through all of these pieces and scrubbing them clean it didn't take me long to realize that almost all of the pinkish and purplish colored heat treated stones, had the repetitive theme of the 'powwow' on them because that's the color of the hues of the setting Pleistocene sun's horizon that was reflecting off of everything in that repetitive theme. The majority of those pieces had microlithic cognitive illusion reflection images of the faces of the Mammoth People trekkers that were gathering around the powwow. They are also seen in the background of the scene when pissed off cursing grandpa and irate grandma desecrate the supine dead warrior brave's war painted white face. When grandma bends over and finishes untangling his nervously grazing palomino horse's rein straps from around his broken neck, she spits on the dead warrior brave's war painted white face, and all of the faces of the Caucasian Mammoth People trekkers that are gathering around the powwow have gossipy and shocked expressions on them. Many of their microlithic heads and faces are seen in the finely crazed cracks of the heat treated stone and they look absolutely real.

Another one of the hunter herder microlithic abstract artist's tricks was to use the jagged fractured edges of the heat treated stone that look like scraper spurs all around the perimeter of the flat cortex side of the stone, as the heads and faces of those gathered trekkers. You see them when the flat cortex side of the stone is at the top of the piece and level with your gaze as if it was the space above their hood and bonnet covered heads. When viewing the sides of the piece in this position, you'll see the perfect silhouette or statuesque images of the characters of the folklore tale that you are viewing. There close-up images follow all of the microlithic abstract art rules. For instance, if you invert the most obvious image of one of the character's heads, they'll morph into another character that they're at 'odds' with.

Another one of the hunter herder microlithic abstract artist's 'techniques' that is fairly common on heat treated stone is the use of smooth and slightly concave surfaces that aren't the cortex surface of the stone but appear to be pecked. These surfaces have the incredible pecked out combined optical and cognitive illusion close-up images of Mammoth People's faces that are best seen at one specific angle. The most important thing that I learned from going through all four 'five gallon' buckets of heat treated stone that was all found on a relatively small area that I know was a 'butcher' site because of its lack of potsherds and because of all of the grey residue that was still stuck on the pieces, is that every single piece has imagery from one of their repetitive themes or folklore tales on it, mostly from the 'volcanic mass exodus'. It's as if they couldn't use a tool if it didn't pay tribute to their ancestors for the trials and tribulations that they went through to get to 'here'.

The Mammoth People hunter herder microlithic abstract arts figurative language has taught me many things about the real world without ever having to leave my home and I didn't learn those things from the internet, rather I used the internet to verify what I was seeing and interpreting off of their microlithic abstract art. Early on in the interpretations, before I had found the Mammoth People themselves, I found imagery of a sturgeon fish that I knew looked like a sturgeon fish but wasn't positive until I looked up sturgeon fish on the internet and saw a picture of them. To my utter amazement, the picture of the side view of the one that I saw on the internet matched the one on the microlithic abstract art right down to the spot on the side of its gill that I had no idea existed until I saw it on the microlithic abstract art. Another instance of being educated by the Mammoth People hunter herder microlithic abstract artist was when I found out that humpback whales had these channels on the underside of their chins and necks. I didn't know what to even call them until I looked it up on the internet which confirmed what I saw, verifying that the Caucasian Mammoth People had hunted humpback whales from their white sea lion covered kayaks with long spears that had bone harpoon like tips. Oh, and those channels, are called 'ventral grooves'. They run from the lower jaw to the umbilicus, about halfway along the underside of the body. It was as if I was seeing the real Ice Age world without ever having to leave my small basement room study...or museum.

Another defining moment that I figured out after having found the Mammoth People and that they had domesticated mammoth, and that they also hunted humpback whales....or more likely their calves, was that the sorceress that came to the quaint cottage to conduct an exorcism on unconscious grandpa, intentionally dressed like the Steller's sea eagle. I had never seen one before and didn't even know they existed, or where they came from until I saw them on a T.V. documentary series called 'Planet Earth'. It was the segment that focused on the volcanic land of Eastern Russia called Kamchatka. Could those Steller's sea eagles have been on the coastal waters near present day Washington State thirteen millennia ago? Probably so, but it's a very good bet that the Mammoth People originated somewhere around the British Isles and migrated east across the Balkans and Russia to the highly volcanic lands of Kamchatka....the land of fire and ice. It was one of those violently erupting volcanoes that chased the Mammoth People out on to the predator sea ice sheet that stretched all the way to present day Washington State. All of the pieces of their epic journey to 'here' came together from a culmination of six years of intensive never ending interpretations giving me a mental picture of the greatest story ever told.

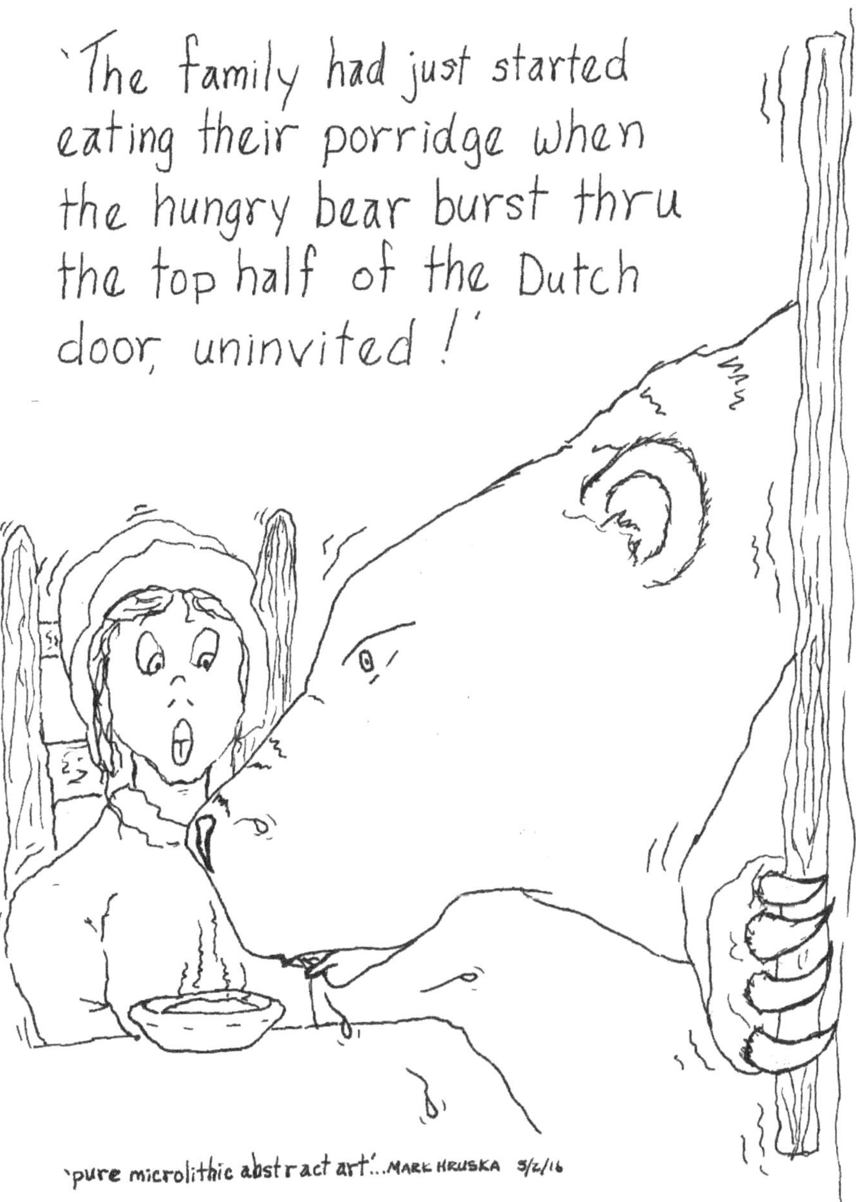

14. The expression on the waist high
young maiden's childlike face says it all…

Chapter Thirteen

Conclusion

It simply comes down to this to describe the Caucasian Mammoth Peoples microlithic abstract art figurative language and how our understanding of the history of the occupation of the North American continent is fundamentally wrong.... As the interpreter of it, you are in their heads imagining the telling of their repetitive epic folklore tales while you visually follow along not by turning the pages of a two dimensional story book, but by turning and rotating the rubbed and etched out three dimensional combined optical and cognitive illusion close-up almost 'statuesque' stone images that are seen from one distinct angle and that have microlithic cognitive or combined optical and cognitive illusion reflection images that appear further away, reflecting off of them, from one scene to the next. They did the same thing with potsherds but they used the tiny pieces of sand aggregate that are embedded in their fractured edges as the further away microlithic reflection images that reflected off of the combined optical and cognitive illusion close-up image that 'is' the whole rubbed and etched out potsherd. Now, imagine that the combined optical and cognitive illusion images are rubbed and etched out 'pareidolia' which is the 'mind's tendency to "recognize" common shapes (especially faces) in random patterns. I can't just call it 'pareidolia' because there's a difference between the optical, the cognitive and the combined optical and cognitive illusion images. The Mammoth People hunter herder microlithic abstract art is based on 'simulacrum'- a perceived image resulting from 'pareidolia', the mind's tendency to "recognize" common shapes (especially faces) in random patterns. The Mammoth People hunter herder microlithic abstract artists rubbed and etched out pareidolia that they saw in the heat treated stone, flint, chert, granite, limestone, siltstone or any other stone that they can see microlithic imagery in or on. They also did the same thing with pottery sherds and bone.

All of us have a finite number of hours to exist on this beautiful planet. A great deal of those hours will be spent trying to make sense of who we are, what we are, when we are and where we are in this vast universe that we inhabit. Only after reaching a pure state of 'rationality' will a lucky few have enough hours left in our short lives to figure out...'why' we are....

Frustratingly, I've come to the conclusion that the reason that no one has ever figured out the microlithic abstract art figurative language is because for one thing...it's extremely difficult to find what you don't know you're looking for. More importantly though, I believe that it's our meticulous scientific methods that have prevented us from discovering the Mammoth Peoples figurative microlithic abstract art language in the first place because using those proven scientific methods the way that 'we' think we should in our real time, prevented us from seeing the microlithic abstract art the way that 'they' actually 'did' see it in their real time. The arrogance of many present day intellectuals 'prevents' them from seeing the bigger picture....this is something that I've been mulling over ever since an extended family member who has a college degree, refused to even look at the microlithic abstract art because he 'just knew' that it couldn't possibly exist, because 'those people' didn't have time to create art on everything that they used because.... "Mark"..."They were too busy trying to survive." Or, how about this emphatic remark made before he looked at any of the evidence that would have verified what I was trying so hard to describe to him, and which he never did see; "You could always right a children's book..." He'll never know how crushing that statement was....or....maybe he did...because this was after I had been working frantically for over five years to verify the existence of the Mammoth People and their nemesis the Palomino Pony People and was trying to do it in the most scientific way that I knew how which was to find a way to verify it as empirical evidence through repetitiveness.

I did that by showing the same imagery and scenes on hundreds of different artifacts from over twenty different sites. In other words, once I found certain characters of a common folklore tale or saw scenes from it on an artifact, I could interpret the rest of the piece predicting what else you'll see on it before ever actually seeing it...how else could I have pieced together their entire folklore tales? When I saw a variation of a repetitive theme and then saw it again and then again, only then could it become part of the whole folklore tale. I interpreted the Mammoth People microlithic abstract art on thousands of pieces until I just wasn't finding any more variations. Only then did I start writing this book to record what I discovered from a lifetime of research. Everything that I've written to describe and interpret the Mammoth People hunter herder microlithic abstract art figurative language has been recorded in 'chronological' order as I discovered and interpreted it in those individual interpretations that I processed. There are over one thousand seven hundred of them to date, but hundreds more that are written up but not processed. The 'descriptions' of all the pieces that I interpreted and processed have about a paragraph length of a brief description in a document that I called 'A Description of the Individual Microlithic Abstract Artworks', describing the piece and the date that I interpreted them and processed them along with their write-up. Those descriptions are a chronology of the discovery of every pieces folklore tale and it documents how I figured out the whole story of every complete epic folklore tale. The dates of the descriptions could be used as a numerical index to assist in finding a piece in the archives which also dates exactly to when I figured out certain aspects of the repetitive themes. And, the summation of each interpreted piece 'is' its title which gives you a good idea of what it's about.

I realized after I finished writing up an interpretation of the jilted forlorn lover and a Mammoth People wedding ceremony that's overseen by a fancifully dressed boisterous magistrate and that shows the bride wearing a long white windblown veil, that that long white windblown veil represents something very significant to the Mammoth People. Two of their most popular folklore tales that demonstrated the epic trials and tribulations that their ancestors went through to get to here, were of the 'volcanic mass exodus' and of the 'powwow'. In the 'volcanic mass exodus' they are chased out of their beloved mountainous homeland by a violently erupting volcano and its pursuing broiling lightning filled ash cloud that chased them over steep rugged mountainous terrain and then down through a narrow windy mountain pass that the dysfunctional lead family was held up in while the multitudes of miserable weary trekkers trudged on around them. After the ordeal with her crotchety grandma, the sobbing waist high young maiden left the front of her compassionate big brother to madly march out in front of him and join the ranks of the other miserable weary trekkers with her cape blowing out behind her, many times with the heads and faces of the multitudes of miserable weary trekkers reflecting off of it.

Then in the second most popular folklore tale of the 'powwow' we saw injured pissed off cursing grandpa hobbling up to the powwow with the windblown horse blanket that was draped over his injured bald head and over his shoulders, blowing out to the side or behind him with the multitudes of miserable weary trekker's heads and faces reflecting off of it. It only makes sense that the brides white veil which we're viewing in much happier times after the Mammoth People trekker's descendants were settled 'here' would represent something that showed respect and acknowledgement to their ancestors who endured those epic trials and tribulations. During the wedding ceremony the multitudes of weddinggoer's heads and faces also reflect off of her long white windblown veil that's being windblown because the ceremony always takes place on a hillside in the springtime. As her veil flaps around during the ceremony it represents a veil or trail of tears that the multitudes of miserable weary ancestors went on to get to 'here'. And the reason that it's white is because the sobbing waist high young maiden's windblown cape hood shows the white faces of the miserable weary trail of trekkers that are being illuminated in the middle of the Pleistocene night by the constant flashes of 'white' lightning from the ash cloud that's pursuing them. Every image that you ever see on their most popular folklore tale of the 'volcanic mass exodus' is being seen because it's being illuminated by a flash of lightning from the roaring broiling volcanic ash cloud.

So it does only make sense that on their wedding day, the bride and groom and everyone else at the wedding would be reminded from the happy brides windblown (imaginary lightning illuminated) white veil, that the young couple will start a new family paying homage to their ancestors for the epic trials and tribulations that they endured in order for them to have the good life that they had and that their children are going to have right 'here'. I thought that that was an excellent analogy and I can honestly say that it's the best conclusion that I can offer after having interpreted so many of the Mammoth Peoples microlithic abstract artworks. I can also conclude that when fully realized, the discovery of the occupancy of the very center of our North American continent over thirteen millennia ago by an extremely capable and intelligent civilized Caucasian culture ultimately has to change the understanding that we have of ourselves in this turbulent fast pace time period. Especially in light of what's being discovered in Turkey at the twelve thousand year old Gobekli Tepe temple site that had been intentionally buried by its occupiers.

The easiest way to explain what I discovered from the microlithic abstract arts figurative language is that before man built megaliths such as the pyramids, Stone Henge and Gobekli Tepe, he lived in an equally mystical 'microlithic' world that seemed to culminate with two distinctly different lithic tool cultures that clashed in the center of the North American continent over thirteen thousand years ago. The Palomino Pony People (known as the Clovis People to present day archaeology) made their large Clovis type spear points and their stone tools to be functional, symmetrical and aesthetically pleasing to the eye whereas the Caucasian Mammoth People created their stubby girthy looking spear points and their reduced looking stone tools to not only be tough and utilitarian friendly but to also incorporate rubbed and etched out images and scenes. Scenes from one of their many popular repetitive themes, or folklore tales, that taught their children about the trials and tribulations that their ancestors experienced on their epic journey to 'here' after they were chased out of their beloved mountainous homeland by a violently erupting volcano and its broiling thunderously roaring male lion lightning filled ash cloud that relentlessly pursued them and drove them out onto the predator ice sheet. And after countless trials and tribulations including the ones that took place as their miserable and weary multitudes trekked across the windswept prairie, they ended up right 'here' from whence I record their epic journey....the original... 'Greatest Story Ever Told'.

......"it just is what it is"....Mark Hruska

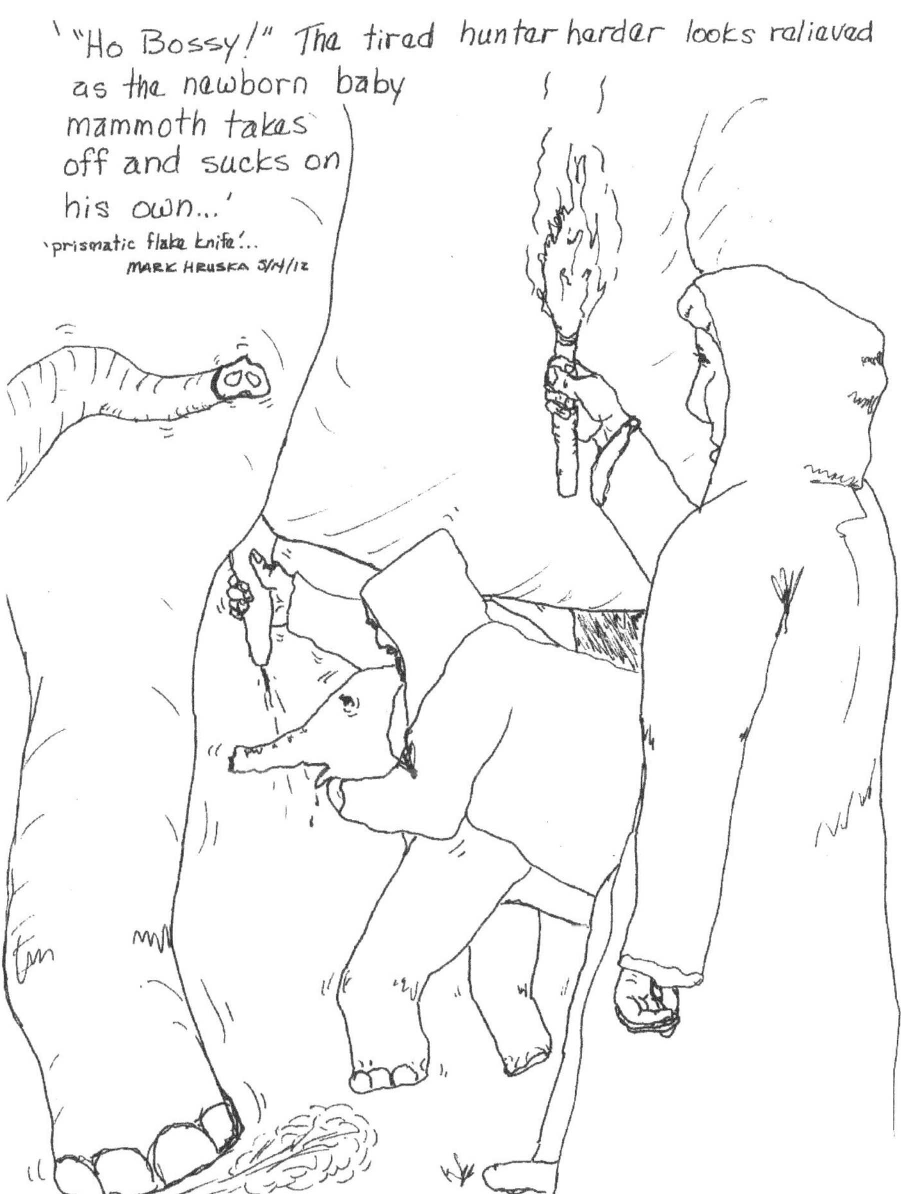

15. Sheep, cattle, and human birth could all be
difficult but the mammoth birth was especially difficult
for dad who then had to get the clumsy newborn to nurse.

Glossary

Awl: a pointed instrument used for piercing small holes

Cognitive illusion: cognitive illusions are assumed to be an interaction based on assumptions about the world which lead to unconscious inferences an idea first suggested in the 19th century by Hermann Helmholz.

Debitage: The collective term used by archaeologists to refer to the sharp-edged lithic waste material left over when someone creates a stone tool.

Dorsal: Directed toward or situated on the back surface as opposed to the ventral.

Dutch door: A door consisting of two units horizontally divided so that each half can be opened or closed separately.

Gobekli Tepe: "Potbelly hill" in Turkey, is a twelve thousand year old megalithic temple or worship site found buried in Turkey that's changing archaeologist's world view of ancient hunter gatherer peoples as an advanced culture upending the conventional view of the rise of civilization.

Medium: The material or technique with which an artist works.

Optical illusion: (also called a visual illusion) is an illusion caused by the visual system and characterized by visually perceived images that differ from objective reality.

Provenance: The source and ownership of a work of art or an archaeological find.

Sentient: adjective 1. having the power of perception by the senses; consciousness.
2. characterized by sensation and consciousness.

noun   1. a person or thing that is sentient
2. the conscious mind.

Ventral: Directed toward or situated on the front or the belly surface; opposite of dorsal

Interpretation Example #1

Date: 8/23/17

Interpreter: Mark Hruska

Reference Number: 20170001

Description of Artifact: '5a, school site' 'Paleo Amerind (Mammoth People) heat treated flint debitage pure microlithic abstract art'.

Short Description: 'pure microlithic abstract art'... '...you are viewing the statuesque image of the decrepit elderly herdswoman as perceived by the 'madly marching' waist high young maiden!'

Photographs:

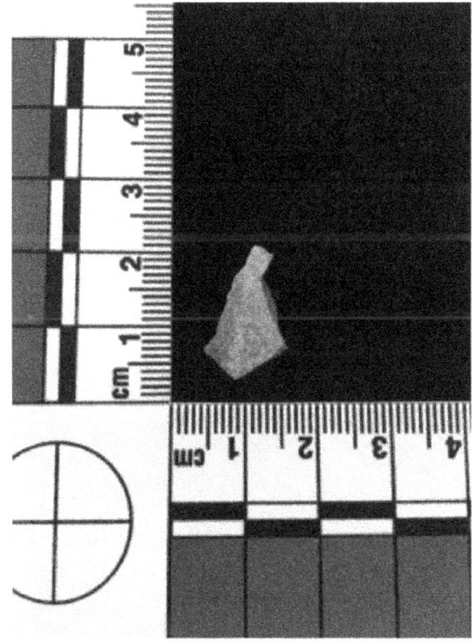

1.a 20170001

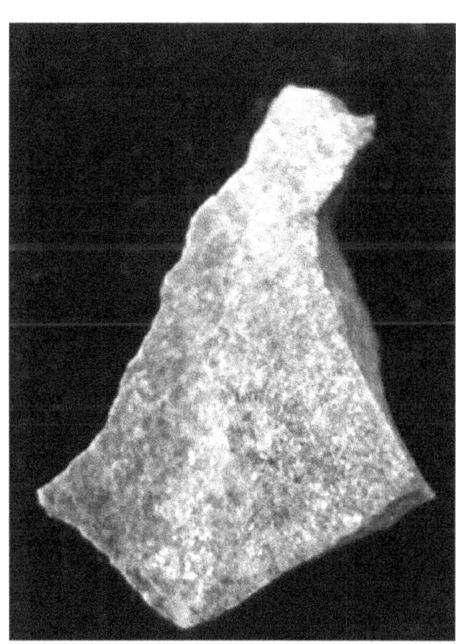

1.b 20170001

Interpretation:

This piece of heat treated flint debitage has been transformed into a fantastic statuesque image of the decrepit elderly herdswoman that the waist high young maiden is 'madly marching' towards in the Mammoth People's repetitive theme or epic folklore tale of the 'volcanic mass exodus'. The decrepit elderly herdswoman is leaning forward on her cane as she trudges along with the ranks of other miserable weary trekkers who are coming down through the narrow windy mountain pass in the middle of the Pleistocene night. They are going around the waist high young maiden's dysfunctional lead family who is held up in the middle of the narrow pass. I'm not going to go through that whole epic folklore tale but I am going to describe what can readily be seen on this fantastic microlithic abstract artwork. Start out by viewing the smooth flat ventral side of the piece and have the narrow end of it at the top. Then rotate the piece slightly clockwise until the narrow end is pointing to about the one-o-clock position, as if it were the hour hand on a Pleistocene clock. Once in this position, put on your 'mind's eye' goggles and peer intently at the tiny masterpiece. When you do, you'll be viewing the most incredible microlithic combined optical and cognitive illusion statuesque lightning illuminated image of the right side view of the whole decrepit elderly herdswoman. She has her cape hood or shawl over her bonnet and over her shoulders. It's encompassing the right side of her white face. You can even see how the frilled front edge of her bonnet is sticking out from under the front of it over her forehead. The cape is concealing her arms and the cane that her right one is holding and leaning on. She's hunched over as her rubbed out right shoulder indicates. You are viewing her during a flash of lightning from the violently erupting volcanoes ash cloud that's pursuing the fleeing Mammoth People. In fact, you can almost see the grey ash that's falling like snow and that's superimposed on her. To verify that this is indeed how the crying waist high young maiden perceives her when she turned away from her compassionate big brother to start 'marching' towards the ranks of other miserable weary trekkers, simply bring the right edge of the piece or the front of the decrepit elderly herdswoman, towards your gaze and use a magnifier to zoom in and peer intently to just below where her rubbed out white right hand is holding onto the cane. When you do and when your eyes adjust to the subtle differences in the heat treated grey and white flint stone, you'll see the microlithic cognitive illusion reflection image of the front right side view of the 'madly marching' waist high young maiden's lightning illuminated childlike white pug nosed face. Since it's a reverse image of her it's actually a reflection of the front left side of her white face as she rapidly and blindly approaches the decrepit elderly herdswoman from her right. Once you see the 'madly marching' waist high young maiden's white reflection, drop your gaze down to your lower right to see the further away microlithic cognitive illusion reflection image of the front right side view of her compassionate big brother from his waist up. His right shoulder is visible because his right arm, which is actually his left arm, is hanging down while his right one is holding their crotchety grandma's left stretcher pole. That's because he's her front left porter and she's sitting on her special armchair that's attached to that stretcher. He is telling his little sister to hold her head up high because she didn't do anything wrong when crotchety grandma unleashed her tirade on her that ended with her yelling at her to go get her naughty kitty and go 'march' out ahead of her big brother where she could keep a glaring eyeball on the two of them...meaning her and her naughty kitty. The 'madly marching' waist high young maiden is looking back over her right shoulder towards her compassionate big brother instead of watching where she was blindly marching to. To verify further, simply bring the front of the decrepit elderly herdswoman, towards your gaze and then onto your left until you are viewing the rough looking dorsal side of the artwork. Rotate it so that that narrow end is again pointing to the one-o-clock position. Once in this position, you will once again be viewing the right side view of the decrepit elderly herdswoman and even see more of the front right side view of her old face. And if you want to be sure that it's her, simply drop your gaze to below about where her cape covered right arm that's holding the cane, would be. Below that rubbed out ledge which would be the underside of her right arm, you'll see the microlithic cognitive illusion closer-up reflection image of the front right side view of the 'madly marching' waist high young maiden's lightning illuminated childlike white face. Once you see her closer up reflection, you realize that she's rapidly approaching the decrepit elderly herdswoman because your eyes instantly adjust to see the rubbed and etched out reflection image of the front right side view of her childlike face that seems to have a bewildered look on it.

It's just to your lower left of her closer up reflection image. The chin of her closest up image is reflecting off of the hemline of the decrepit elderly herdswoman's long dress. You can clearly see the waist high young maiden's rubbed out cognitive illusion right eye, her pug nose and her slightly downturned mouth that gives her childlike face a bewildered expression. The 'master' microlithic abstract artisan or headmaster of the school does this to show motion. The proto-cinema scene shows two of the same reflection images, one much bigger than the first, in order to demonstrate that the reflection image is getting closer and closer and doing so rapidly. To verify further that it is indeed the hunched over decrepit elderly herdswoman that she's approaching rapidly from the right, bring the front of her or the right edge of the piece, slightly towards your gaze. Then zoom in on the upper mid area of that rubbed out edge. When you do, you'll see the perfect rubbed out microlithic combined optical and cognitive illusion closer up image of the front right side view of the hunched over decrepit elderly herdswoman's old face that has a painful expression on it. It's as if her cane has been knocked out from under her and she's now falling forward. There's always more on these fantastic microlithic abstract artworks, especially the ones that have been created by the headmaster to be used as teaching tools that the students will try to replicate. There's no question about it... when you view the smooth flat ventral side of this piece of supposedly 'debitage'... you are viewing the statuesque image of the decrepit elderly herdswoman as perceived by the 'madly marching' waist high young maiden!

…… "it just is what it is"...Mark Hruska

Interpretation Example #2

Date: 7/31/17

Interpreter: Mark Hruska

Reference Number: 20170002

Description of Artifact: '1g' 'Paleo Amerind (Mammoth People) large flint knife scraper eating utensil'

Short Description: 'pure microlithic abstract art'... 'The decrepit elderly herdswoman and the 'madly marching' waist high young maiden catch only a glimpse of each other before the collision!'

Photograph:

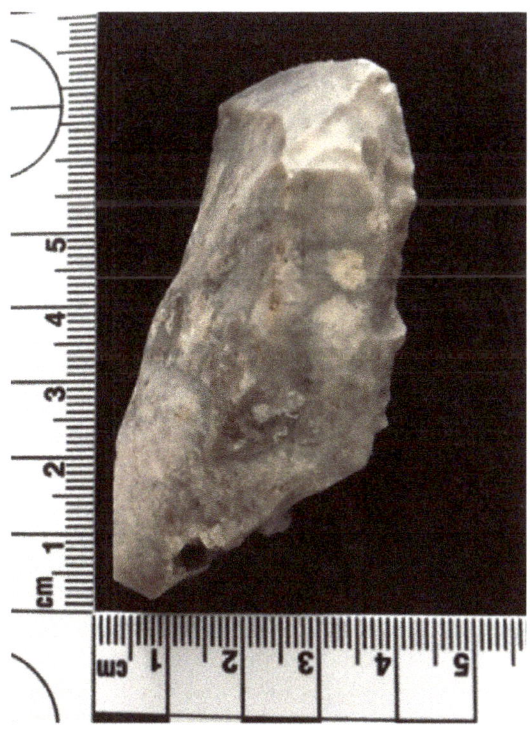

2.a 20170002

Interpretation:

I found this very large flint knife scraper eating utensil this season at the '1g' site that is located at the head of the fork in the river about a half mile north of Ulysses, Nebraska. It's only about a half mile from where I farm. What always amazes me about anything that I find at this location is that even though you don't find much, many of the artifacts that I do find are rather large as if that person that created them was a big man with big hands or that he was someone that specialized in creating big pieces. Up until I found this site I suspected that the Mammoth People measured their microlithic abstract art skill level by being able to create the smallest pieces with the most complete repetitive theme or folklore tales on them. This piece proves that at least one individual could take his microlithic abstract art skills to a larger level and I believe he was able to do it because of the cognitive illusion imagery that he saw 'in' the flint stone that looked like Mammoth People's heads and faces and that was much larger than other imagery that you see in most fossiliferous flint. This unique flint knife scraper eating utensil has scenes from the Mammoth People's most popular repetitive theme or folklore tale of the 'volcanic mass exodus' on it. Those scenes concentrate on the part of the story when the upset waist high young maiden had just finished being consoled by her compassionate teenage big brother who was their crotchety grandma's front left porter. She turned away from him to go 'madly march' out ahead of him per their crotchety grandma's shrieking instructions. He told her to hold her head up high because she didn't do anything wrong. As she madly marched out ahead of him to join the ranks of the multitudes of other miserable weary trekkers who were trudging down through the narrow windy mountain pass and around the held up dysfunctional lead family, she took big marching steps while she swung her little cape covered arms wildly to and fro. As she did so, she also looked down at her naughty kitty to scold him and give him a piece of her own mind for getting her into all that trouble with crotchety grandma. Since she was looking down at him she wasn't paying any attention to where she was madly marching to, that is until she saw the hunched over decrepit elderly herdswoman during a flash of lighting. There was almost a constant flickering of lightning coming from the violently erupting volcanoes broiling ash cloud that was pursuing the fleeing Mammoth People. It lit their way but there were also interludes of darkness where they couldn't see where they were going as they painstakingly made their way over the rough mountainous terrain in the middle of the Pleistocene night...

I started this pieces interpretation with its main scene viewed from one distinct angle which highlights the skill level of the Mammoth People 'master' microlithic abstract artisan who created it. Hold the large flint knife scraper eating utensil with your left hands fingers over a soft cloth so that you don't accidentally break a piece off of it if you were to accidentally drop it on a hard surface. There are a couple of graver spurs on the one long scraper edge that absolutely can't get damaged! As you view the whole piece you'll see that it's pristine other than having some rust stains on and near the dorsal ridge. They were created by a fast moving farm implement and we are extremely fortunate that it didn't destroy this fantastic thirteen millennium year old artwork. Now, view the dorsal side that has that rust stain on the dorsal ridge and have the narrow end of the piece at the bottom. There is a large rounded out hollow fossil hole to the right of it. Have the back of the piece or the ventral side of the piece lying on your left hands fingers with your little finger supporting the piece where that hollow fossil hole is. Your left thumb should be lifted up out of the way so that you can see the entire dorsal side of the piece. Notice that there is a rubbed flat almost triangular shaped area on the edge to your left of the hollow fossil hole and that's towards the inside side of the palm of your left hand. Bring the long scraper edge that has those two distinct graver spurs on it, slightly up towards your gaze until that rubbed flat edge that's near the inside side of the palm of your left hand is flush with your left eyes gaze. Then rotate the piece slightly one way or the other until that flat edge is also vertical to your gaze. Once in this position, put on your 'mind's eye' goggles, take a step back and view the whole piece. When you do, you'll be viewing the combined optical and cognitive illusion close-up statuesque image of the right side view of the 'madly marching' waist high young maiden's head that has her cape hood over her bonnet. Her surprised looking childlike faces pug nose is the bigger graver spur that's on that scraper edge to your right, and the tiny one below it to your lower right 'is' her pouty bottom lip. You are seeing her during a flash of lightning which is also illuminating her wide opened teary right eye that is a white fossil. Once you see her as she turns her head away from your gaze to look towards the decrepit elderly herdswoman that she's about to blindly run into, take a step back, readjust your gaze and view the whole piece again, but this time imagine in your 'mind's eye' that you are actually viewing the combined optical and cognitive illusion close-up statuesque image of the front right side view of the decrepit elderly herdswoman's head and right shoulder. That's right....you are also viewing her as she turns her head to her right to look down past the front of her right shoulder to briefly see the 'madly marching' waist high young maiden about to blindly collide with her. The rubbed flat edge of the piece is the back of her hunched over right shoulder and it helps you visualize that she is hunched over leaning on her cane that's being held with her right hand. She has a cape hood over her bonnet too and she is sharing the back of her head with the 'madly marching' waist high young maiden's head because they are 'opposing heads' and are in effect 'in' each other's heads thinking horrifically of each other during this miserable moment in Pleistocene time. What's even more intriguing is that they also share one of their wide opened horrified looking lightning illuminated eyes a Pleistocene second before the collision. The decrepit elderly herdswoman's wide opened lightning illuminated left eye is also the 'madly marching' waist high young maiden's wide opened lightning illuminated right eye. Once you focus on the decrepit elderly herdswoman's head and horrified looking old face that's turned to her right and towards your gaze, you'll instantly be able to focus on her cognitive illusion horrified looking right eye, the bridge of her nose that's on the dorsal ridge of the piece where the farm implement rust stain is, and most importantly, you'll be able to focus on her opened mouth that shows her top two middle white snaggleteeth projecting out of it. Her two middle bottom teeth appear to be missing and her opened old mouth is directly to your left of the waist high young maiden's pouty mouth's lips the bottom of which is the tiny graver spur that's on the scraper edge of the artwork. To verify all of this we should be able to use a magnifier and zoom in and see microlithic cognitive illusion reflection images of both of them reflecting off of each other. To start lets zoom in on their shared wide opened lightning illuminated white fossil eye. When you imagine that it's the decrepit elderly herdswoman's horrified looking left eye, you'll clearly see the microlithic cognitive illusion reflection image of the side view of the 'madly marching' waist high young maiden's head. The front of her childlike white pug nosed face is on the right edge of it and it looks exactly like the close-up image of her that's rubbed and etched out on the right scraper edge of the piece. In fact, the hunter herder microlithic 'master' abstract artisan who created this artwork saw that image in the stone and then created the much larger closer up statuesque image of her around it. It's as if you could zoom in and see her faraway reflection image much closer up by simply taking a step back and viewing the whole piece. You can also see the microlithic cognitive illusion reflection image of the whole right side of her 'madly marching' body below her lightning illuminated white face. Her right shoulder and forward swinging right arm are reflecting off of the decrepit elderly herdswoman's left cheek, and her long dress covered left leg is rubbed out taking a big 'marching' step forward. Once you see her reflection off of the decrepit elderly herdswoman's left eye and left cheek, readjust your gaze and assume that you are now viewing the close-up image of the right side view of the 'madly marching' waist high young maiden's head. Then zoom in on the darker purplish center area of the piece that is just to your left of the decrepit elderly herdswoman's nose and adjacent to your upper left of her opened mouth and top two middle white snaggleteeth. When you do, you'll see the microlithic cognitive illusion reflection image of the front right side view of the decrepit elderly herdswoman's whole hunched over body with her head turned to her right towards your gaze. Peer intently at her head, face and right shoulder and you'll see that it's the exact same image of her that you see when you take a step back and view the whole piece! You can even see the whitish fossil spot on the front of her left shoulder that mimics the hollow fossil hole on the much closer up image of her. Perhaps it represents a tear in her cape or shawl. All around her reflection image are the multitudes of other miserable weary Mammoth People trekkers who are funneling down through the narrow windy mountain pass and splitting to either side of the dysfunctional lead family that's held up in the middle of the pass. To your left on the top of the decrepit elderly herdswoman's right shoulder is the awesome microlithic cognitive illusion closer-up reflection image of the front right side view of a herdswoman's lightning illuminated sorrowful looking white face. This reflection image is another reflection image of the decrepit elderly herdswoman herself that's closer up and reflecting off of the 'madly marching' waist high young maiden as she gets closer and closer to her. The Mammoth People hunter herder microlithic abstract artist does this to show motion and it demonstrates their ability to create proto-cinema. Once you see this proto-cinema scene, move your gaze to the upper left part of their shared hoods or shawls to see the front right side views of at least seven or eight trekkers heads and faces as they trudge along down through the narrow windy mountain pass. The top part of their shared hoods or shawls that are over their bonnets also has the microlithic cognitive illusion reflection images of the front right side views of the further away multitudes of Mammoth People trekkers heads and faces as they descend through the narrow windy mountain pass. Now, to verify that the 'madly marching' waist high young maiden did indeed blindly run into the decrepit elderly herdswoman and knock her cane out from under her causing her to fall face first on to the rough rocky terrain, we should be able to see the two of them inverted to one another because they would be at 'odds' with each other. So do this, slowly rotate the artwork counterclockwise as if the 'madly marching' waist high young maiden suddenly looks upward to your upper right. Keep going until her head is inverted and the reflection in her wide opened upside down right eye 'morphs' into the microlithic cognitive illusion reflection image of the left side view of her own lightning illuminated childlike white face that's looking to your upper left as if she were startled and looking towards the decrepit elderly herdswoman that she has just blindly ran into. This means that her reflection has to be reflecting off of the decrepit elderly herdswoman that she has just ran into, so take a step back, readjust your gaze and view the whole piece, concentrating on the rubbed flat edge that's now to your upper right and that was previously the back of the close-up image of the hunched over decrepit elderly herdswoman's right shoulder. When you do, you'll realize that the whole piece has morphed into the combined optical and cognitive illusion further away statuesque image of the front right side view of the 'whole' hunched over decrepit elderly herdswoman as she leans forward on her cane and hobbles along. She's turning her head to her right to look down past her right shoulder a Pleistocene instant before the 'madly marching' waist high young maiden blindly runs into her. The front right side view of her old face is flat but it has her left eye, her nose and her mouth rubbed out. Zoom in to the brighter white lightning illuminated area of her right cheek, just to your lower left of her cognitive illusion right eye. When you do, you'll see the microlithic cognitive illusion fairly close-up reflection image of the front view of the waist high young maiden's surprised looking lightning illuminated childlike white face. To further verify that they have just collided and that the decrepit elderly herdswoman is falling face first towards the rocky ground after the waist high young maiden knocked the cane that she was holding with her right hand out from under her, simply rotate the artwork clockwise as if the decrepit elderly herdswoman is now falling face first towards the rocky ground. Have the front right side view of her flat face facing towards you as if she were now actually laying on the rocky ground and that it is the rocky ground that is creating the concave impression image on the ventral side of the artwork that 'is' now her statuesque body that's lying on the ground with the multitudes of miserable weary Mammoth People trekkers gathering around her and the mortified waist high young maiden. You'll clearly see all of the microlithic cognitive illusion reflection images of their fairly close-up heads and faces reflecting off of this side of the fallen decrepit elderly herdswoman's prone body that's towards your gaze. To verify further that the decrepit elderly herdswoman is now lying prone on the rocky hard landscape with her head turned to her right towards the mortified waist high young maiden who sees her like you now see her, slowly bring the top of her fallen body's cape or shawl covered head towards your gaze from your right. Lift it up slightly so that you can see who or what is reflecting off of it from an extremely close up position. When you do, you'll see the incredible rubbed out image of the front and mostly right side view of the waist high young maiden's naughty kitty's face. That's right! He was briskly walking alongside and slightly ahead of her when she blindly ran into the decrepit elderly herdswoman and knocked her down with her head hitting the rock hard ground right in front of him. You can't miss his rubbed out squinting left cat eye that is actually his right one because it's a reflection. His cat nose is to your lower left of it and his cat mouth is below it. You can even see a whisker rubbed out below his squinting eye. The whole piece should be resting on your left hands thumb as if it were the rocky terrain that the fallen decrepit elderly herdswoman is now lying on. Once you see the kitty's face reflecting off of the top of the fallen decrepit elderly herdswoman's head, you will have no problem realizing that he is also an opposing head to her because he is sharing the back of his head with hers too, just as he is with his mortified waist high young maiden who was just giving him a piece of her own mind and not paying any attention to where she was 'madly marching' to. To verify that, simply lower his face and the inverted fallen decrepit elderly herdswoman's head to see the opposing head to both of them of the mortified waist high young maiden and the close-up right side view image of her that we started the interpretation with. Then bring the front of her mortified pug nosed childlike face towards your gaze and then onto your left as if you wanted to see the other side or the left side of her head. Once in this position, zoom in and peer intently at the rubbed out concave center part of this ventral side of the artwork. When you do, you'll see a rubbed out microlithic cognitive illusion reflection scene of the fallen decrepit elderly herdswoman with the multitudes of other miserable weary trekkers gathered all around her. They're reflecting off of this whole side of the mortified waist high young maiden's head. It seems that the clearest ones are near the bottom along the front of her neck. Just zoom in and peer intently until they come into focus. It's mostly the front right side views of their lightning illuminated heads and faces. Once you see this last scene of the folklore tale, turn the mortified waist high young maiden's head around to see the right side view of her when she was still blindly 'madly marching' towards the ranks of the miserable weary Mammoth People trekkers before the incident took place. She was giving her naughty kitty a piece of her own mind and making him walk instead of carrying him because of all the trouble he had gotten her into with crotchety grandma. As she did so, she was rapidly approaching the unsuspecting decrepit elderly herdswoman who only had a Pleistocene second to turn her head to her right to see what was coming. The decrepit elderly herdswoman and the 'madly marching' waist high young maiden catch only a glimpse of each other before the collision!

…… "it just is what it is"….Mark Hruska

Interpretation Example #3

Date: 9/13/17

Interpreter: Mark Hruska

Reference Number: 20170003

Description of Artifact: '1c, hump'... 'Paleo Amerind (Mammoth People) heat treated stone debitage pure microlithic abstract art'

Short Description: 'pure microlithic abstract art'... 'The reflection of the gruff chief's windswept headdress is reflecting off of the statuesque sniffing majestic male lions exposed left canines!'

Photographs:

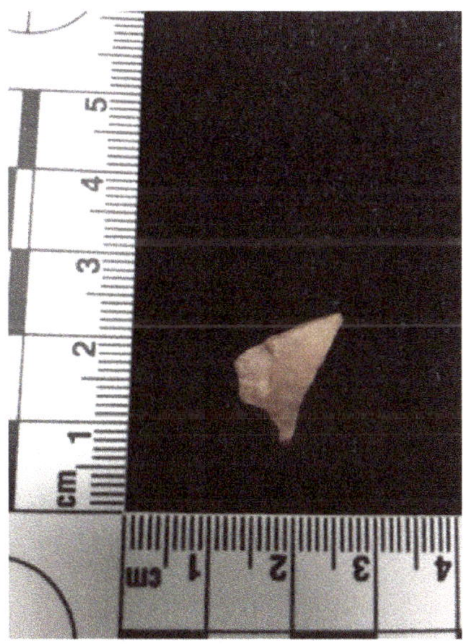

3.a 20170003

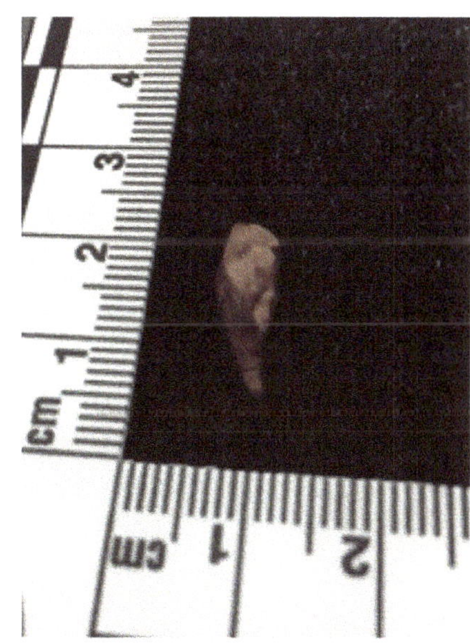

3.b 20170003

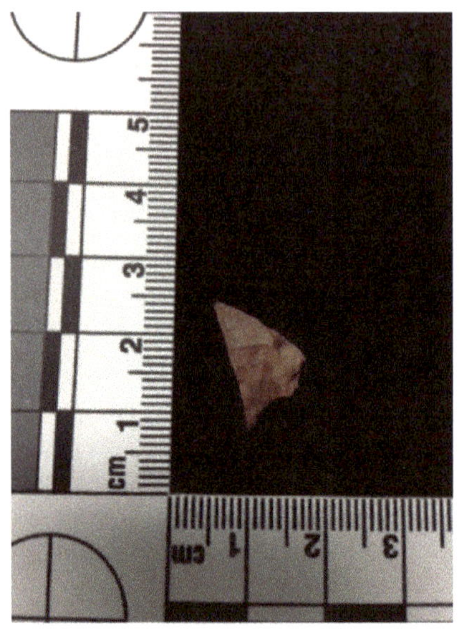

3.c 20170003

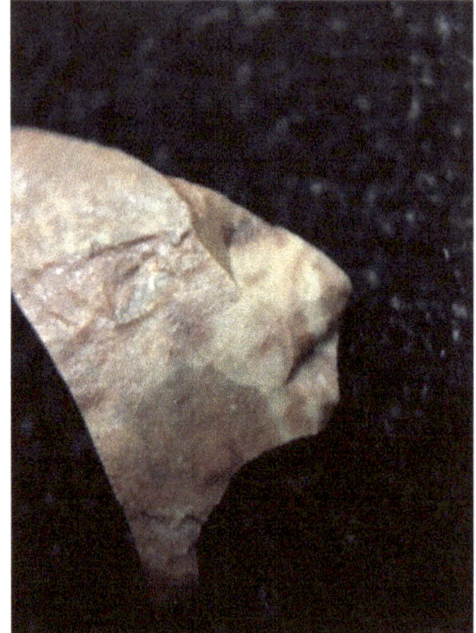

3.d 20170003

Interpretation:

This fantastic Mammoth People microlithic abstract artwork has scenes from their repetitive theme or folklore tale of the 'powwow' on it. It was created out of heat treated stone, not flint. The reddish brown, almost purplish colors within it are conducive to the reflective hues of the setting Pleistocene suns horizon that are cast over the characters of the folklore tale. During this scene the lead hunter herder or 'dad' is standing face to face with the gruff chief in front of the nervous lead mammoth waiting to have their speechless powwow. Up behind dad and sitting on her special armchair atop the nervous lead mammoth is his irate elderly mother who is leaning forward to yell down instructions to everyone over the head of the nervous lead mammoth. She was just yelling at her panting fair young maiden granddaughter to hold her little brother close to the front of her and stand right next to their lead hunter herder dad because he has a big spear. Now she's yelling down at her to run over and assist her injured cursing grandpa who's hobbling up to the powwow. He was bounced off of his travois when the horse that his fair young maiden granddaughter was riding was spooked by the whooping and hollering Palomino Pony People warrior braves. While all of this was transpiring the excited waist high young lad who was standing directly in front of the gruff chief and next to the right side of his dad, was alerted to a majestic male lion that was up on a ledge to the right of the nervous lead mammoth. He was alerted to him by the gruff chief's fine palomino horse that was snorting and shaking his head up and down while he looked up to his left towards the large predator. At some point the excited waist high young lad managed to get the gruff chief, his stern dad, irate grandma, injured grandpa, his big sister and the rest of the Mammoth People trekkers who were gathering around the powwow, to look up behind them at the majestic male lion that was lounging on the ledge to the upper right of the lead mammoth. He was lying on his belly with his forelegs out in front of him and his head erect. In past interpretations he is usually seen licking off one of his forelegs paws because he had just finished a big meal that was most likely of horse, but this time he seems to be sniffing the breeze that has the scent of horse....

To view the first scene of this interpretation, carefully hold the small piece of what appears to be heat treated stone debitage, with your left hand's fingers. You'll see that the piece has two rubbed flat edges or 'backed' edges that come together at a point. Opposite that point is a short concave edge that is a honed sharp knife edge. The piece is bifacial and that concave knife edge is honed from both sides equally. You could hold the piece by pinching the two rubbed flat or 'backed' edges between your index finger and thumb in order to slice something with that honed sharp short concave or crescent shaped cutting edge. It could also be used like a seam ripper tool. That being said, the whole piece was created as a microlithic abstract artwork first that would then be used as a utilitarian tool or possibly a child's eating utensil. Having scenes from their epic folklore tales on all of their utilitarian tools or eating utensils is how the storytelling Mammoth People related to their children the epic trials and tribulations that their ancestors endured and how they got to 'here' from whence I wright this interpretation. Now, look closely at the honed sharp crescent shaped cutting edge and you'll see that one end of it is long and narrow. Have that long narrow end at the bottom as you look straight towards the honed sharp concave knife edge. Then turn it to your right so that you can view the crescent shape of the concave knife edge. Then rotate the piece clockwise until that long narrow end is at the bottom of the piece resting on your left thumb while the underside of your left index finger rests on the top point where the two 'backed' edges come together. Then the longest rubbed flat 'backed' edge should be to your left and be flush and vertical to your gaze. Once in this positon, put on your 'mind's eye' goggles, take a step back and view the whole piece while you slowly bring the right edge of it towards your gaze. As it swings towards your gaze, you'll be viewing what everyone around the powwow sees when they look up on the ledge that the excited waist high young lad is pointing towards. You'll be viewing the most amazing combined optical and cognitive illusion further away 'statuesque' image of the lounging majestic male lion's head. Before you brought his licking muzzle towards your gaze, you were viewing the perfect right side view of it that shows his bushy mane being blown back in the stiff Pleistocene wind. Then as you bring the front of his panting face towards your gaze, you see the perfect statuesque image of the front view of him. His eyebrows accentuate his statuesque face perfectly. Then as you turn his panting muzzle to your left, you see the perfect statuesque image of the left side of his head. His three dimensional fairly faraway image is so realistic and it's absolutely unbelievable...try to keep in mind that you are viewing him from thirteen millennia in the future. Once you get over the shock of seeing him up there on that ledge like a modern day Sphinx, the way that all of those that were gathered around the powwow did, turn his panting muzzle over to your right so that you can view the right side of his majestic head. Once in this position, take a step back, readjust your gaze and view the whole piece. Stare lazily at it and eventually, you'll see it morph into the combined optical and cognitive illusion close-up image of the front right side view of the excited waist high young lad's head and white face that's looking to your upper right towards the majestic male lion. His mouth and chin are shared with the majestic male lions because they are sharing the backs of their heads and are in effect 'in' each other's heads thinking of each other, but also looking towards each other at the angle that you see both of them. The excited waist high young lad's mouth and his cognitive illusion eyes give his face an expression of astonishment and worriedness. The crescent shaped knife edge is the invisible top edge of his right shoulder that he's looking up over as he stands next to the right side of his dad and directly in front of the gruff chief and his agitated palomino horse. If you use a magnifier to zoom in on the darker area of his summertime cap that's shared with the majestic male lions mane hair, you'll see several further away microlithic cognitive illusion images of the front views of the Mammoth People trekkers heads and faces who are gathered around the powwow.   But let's concentrate on one in particular that's reflecting off of the majestic male lions head because we know that the waist high young lad is directly in front of the gruff chief and that he's trying to get the gruff chief and his stern dad to look to where he's pointing. So use your magnifier to zoom in and peer intently to his loudly talking mouth and chin that he shares with the majestic male lions slightly opened mouth and his chin. In fact, do this. Rotate the male lion's statuesque head slightly counterclockwise as if he raised his sniffing muzzle to get a sniff of tantalizing palomino horse. When his forehead and the bridge of his nose is horizontal to your gaze at the top of the piece, zoom in and peer intently at the front right side of his opened mouth and chin. Just stare at it until your eyes adjust to the micro level of rubbed and etched out art that's on it and that the talented hunter herder microlithic abstract artist was seeing without the aid of magnification. When they do, you'll see the perfect microlithic combined optical and cognitive illusion faraway reflection image of the right side view of the gruff chief's windswept eagle feather headdress covered head and red skinned face that's looking up directly at the front of the majestic male lion's sniffing muzzle. So if they're looking directly towards each other, slowly bring the front of the majestic male lion's sniffing snout towards your gaze all the while keeping your eyes on the gruff chief's white eagle feather headdress that's being blown back over his left shoulder and away from your gaze by the stiff Pleistocene prairie wind. Once you're looking straight at the sniffing majestic male lion from below his chin, turn him a little further to your left so that you are viewing him the way that the gruff chief sees him from down below and in front of him. From this angle, you'll see that the gruff chief's windblown eagle feather headdress is reflecting off of the sniffing majestic male lion's exposed top and bottom individual canine teeth! Now that you've seen this fantastic image of the lounging majestic male lion, I'll take you around the rotational change-up microlithic abstract masterpiece and point out other imagery and scenes. So in the Mammoth People microlithic abstract art figurative language, one of the rules is that 'opposing heads' that are at 'odds' with each other should be inverted to each other. So view the left side of the majestic male lion's statuesque sniffing head. Then rotate it clockwise until it's inverted and the narrow end of the piece is pointing upward at the top of the piece. Once in this position, zoom in and peer intently to that narrow tip. Just stare at it until your eyes adjust to the subtle differences in the reddish brown and cream colored stone. When they do, you'll be viewing the microlithic combined optical and cognitive illusion faraway image of the front right side view of injured cursing grandpa who's hobbling up to the powwow with the brown windblown horse blanket draped over his injured bald head and over his shoulders. It had been nicely covering him before he was bounced off of his travois. You can clearly see how the stiff prairie wind is blowing it out behind him. Once you see his cursing bearded face that's encompassed by the brown horse blanket, move your gaze down to about his waist level to see the cognitive illusion image of the right side view of his concerned fair young maiden granddaughter superimposed on him as she runs up to assist him. The hunter herder microlithic abstract artist may have tried to rub out a second image of her in the deep rub which shows the front left side view of her whole body and sunlit white face. She always has the expression of concern on her childlike face. Notice that injured cursing grandpa's head is an inverted opposing head to the gruff chief who's reflecting off of the inverted majestic male lion's chin and that they are the same size, meaning that they are the same distance from the sniffing majestic male lion. To take the inverted opposing heads rule one step further, simply bring the right edge of the piece which is the front and underside of the chin of the inverted sniffing majestic male lion's head, towards your gaze and then onto your left as if you wanted to see the other side of it or as if you wanted to see the other side of injured cursing grandpa's head that's at the top of the piece. When you do, you'll see that faraway injured grandpa morphs into the microlithic combined optical and cognitive illusion opposing image to him of the left side view of his concerned fair young maiden who's running over to assist him. You can actually see her concerned face that's encompassed by her red capes hood even though it's somewhat blurry from this distance. The stiff prairie wind is blowing her red cape out behind her as she runs towards him. This is amusing to see but what will really grab your attention is when you take a step back and view the whole piece. When you do, you'll be viewing the combined optical and cognitive illusion extremely close-up image of the left side view of the fair young maiden's concerned looking pug nosed childlike face as if she were looking to your upper left towards her injured cursing grandpa's face. The backed edge of the piece that's to your right, and that is also the back of her faraway image, is now the invisible front edge of her red cape hood that's over her bonnet and encompassing the left side of her childlike face. It's as if you could zoom in and see her faraway concerned looking childlike face by simply taking a step back and viewing the whole piece! To verify that it is indeed her childlike face that's looking up towards someone or something, simply zoom in on the front of her mouth and chin to see a rubbed and etched out microlithic reflection image that she's looking towards. Just stare until your eyes adjust to the subtle differences in the heat treated reddish and cream colored heat treated stone. When they do, you won't see her grandpa's reflection, but you will see her irate grandma's reflection as she yells down at her. You'll be viewing the microlithic combined optical and cognitive illusion reflection image of the front left side view of her sunlit head that has her cape hood over her bonnet and that's encompassing her beet red mad face that's glaring down over the head of the nervous lead mammoth. Her face is beet red because she's so mad at the gruff chief and his taunting warrior brave. But get this. Her reflection is a direct inverted opposing head to the gruff chief's faraway reflection that's directly above her on the concerned fair young maiden's nose. Her nose 'is' also the inverted sniffing majestic male lion's chin that has the gruff chief's faraway reflection reflecting off of it that's the same size as irate grandma's reflection. And the fair young maiden is also an inverted opposing head to the sniffing majestic male lion because she's afraid of him...just like she's afraid of the gruff chief and his Palomino Pony People warrior braves, especially the taunting one that had chased her up to the powwow and then sat on his high horse and made jeering gestures at her. That was going on when she had just ran up to the powwow and irate grandma was yelling at her to hold her little brother close to the front of her and stand right next to their stern lead hunter herder dad. To reinforce this last scene that has the extremely close-up image of the left side view of her concerned childlike face that's looking to your upper left towards her irate grandma, simply bring the rubbed flat 'backed' edge of the piece that is also the invisible outline of the front left edge of her red cape hood that's over her bonnet, towards your gaze and stare straight at it. Once in this position, peer intently at it, concentrating on the lower right part of it. Just stare until your eyes adjust to the subtle differences in the mostly Caucasian flesh tone colored stone. When they do, you'll see the incredible cognitive illusion fairly close-up image of the front right side view of the fair young maiden's childlike face that's looking to your upper right towards her yelling irate grandma. And to see her, simply move your gaze to the top narrow end of the piece above the fair young maiden's childlike Caucasian face to see the cognitive illusion image of the front of irate grandma from about the waist up. The front left half of her face is in the narrowest part of the point and the left side of her irate face is encompassed by her cape hood that's over her bonnet. Her cognitive illusion left arm and hand is raised because she's pointing out towards injured cursing grandpa where she wants the fair young maiden to run to and assist him. We know this because his faraway image is on the left side of irate grandma's head making them opposing heads that are 'in' each other's heads thinking deeply of one another! All of this imagery of cursing grandpa, irate yelling grandma and the panting concerned fair young maiden are all inverted opposing heads to the sniffing majestic male lion and the reflection of the gruff chief that's reflecting off of his sniffing muzzles chin. That's because both the lion and the gruff chief are seen as predators to the Mammoth People. To verify that, take another look at the statuesque image of the front of the sniffing majestic male lion's face that actually looks somewhat angry. As the front left side of his angry looking sniffing face comes into view from your right, you see the gruff chief's windblown eagle feather headdress sort of morph into part of the sniffing lions face. The reflection of the gruff chief's windswept headdress is reflecting off of the statuesque sniffing majestic male lions exposed left canines!

...... "it just is what it is"...Mark Hruska

Interpretation Examples #4 (misc.)

Here is an example of the Mammoth Peoples limestone microlithic abstract art. It is the combined optical and cognitive illusion close-up statuesque sunlit image of the right side view of irate grandma as she bends over to untangle the fine palomino horses rein straps from around his dead warrior braves broken neck. It's on the dorsal side of the artwork that's shaped like a prismatic knife, which also happens to be the shape of the snorting horse's snout that's jerking up away from her when she spit on his supine dead riders war painted white face.....

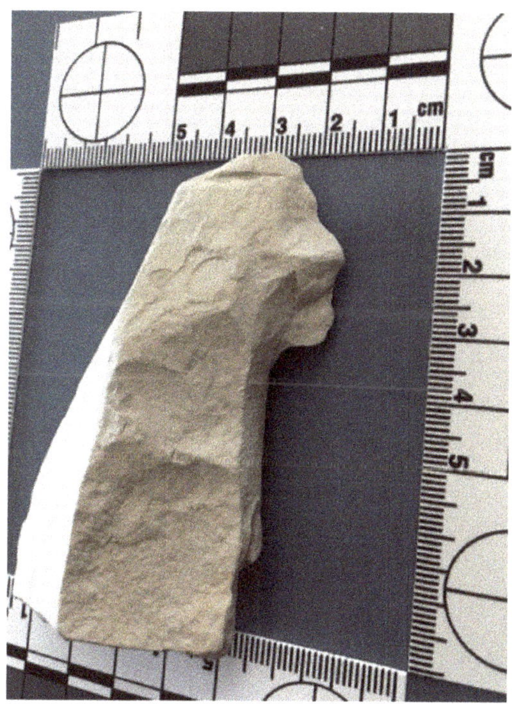

4.a 20170004 (misc.)

Here is the left side view of her bent over image that's on the ventral side of the artwork.....

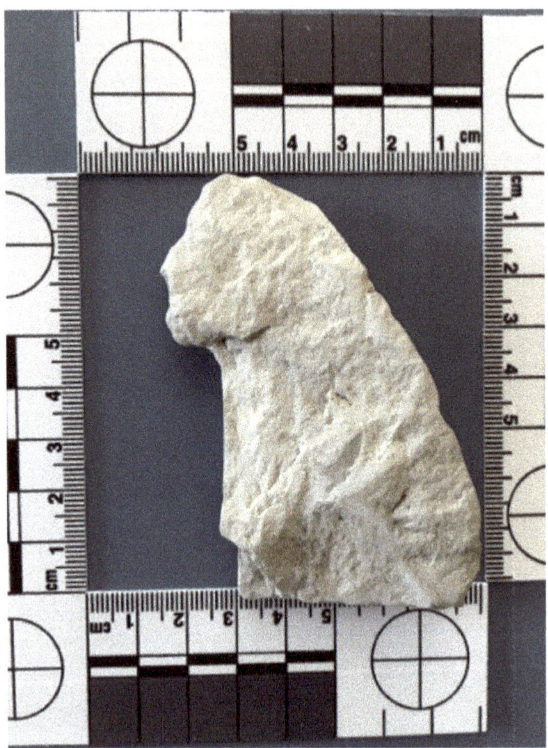

4.b 20170004 (misc.)

Here's another example of the combined optical and cognitive illusion close-up image of the right side view of irate grandma's sunlit head. You will also see the combined optical and cognitive illusion close-up reflection image of the front right side view of her fair young maiden's head and childlike white face reflecting off of the front right side of irate grandma's windblown cape or shawl that's blowing up over her bonnet in the stiff Pleistocene prairie wind. The fair young maiden's childlike faces mouth is rubbed out wide opened giving her an abhorrent expression when she saw her irate grandma spit on the supine dead warrior braves war painted white face.....

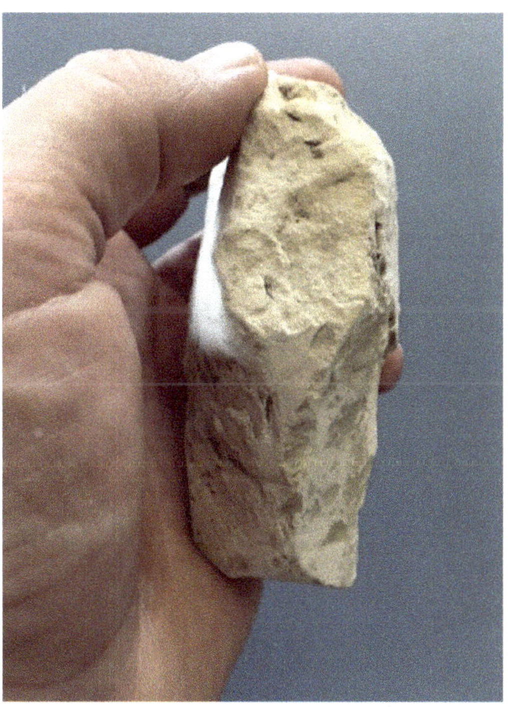

4.c 20170004 (misc.)

Parting thoughts...

I'll leave you with this next image of how far the Laurentide Ice Sheet advanced southward during the last glacial maximum of the North American Continent. It provides a rational reason for why the Mammoth People ultimately settled in the bountiful hydrologic river valley near present day Ulysses in Butler County, Nebraska....

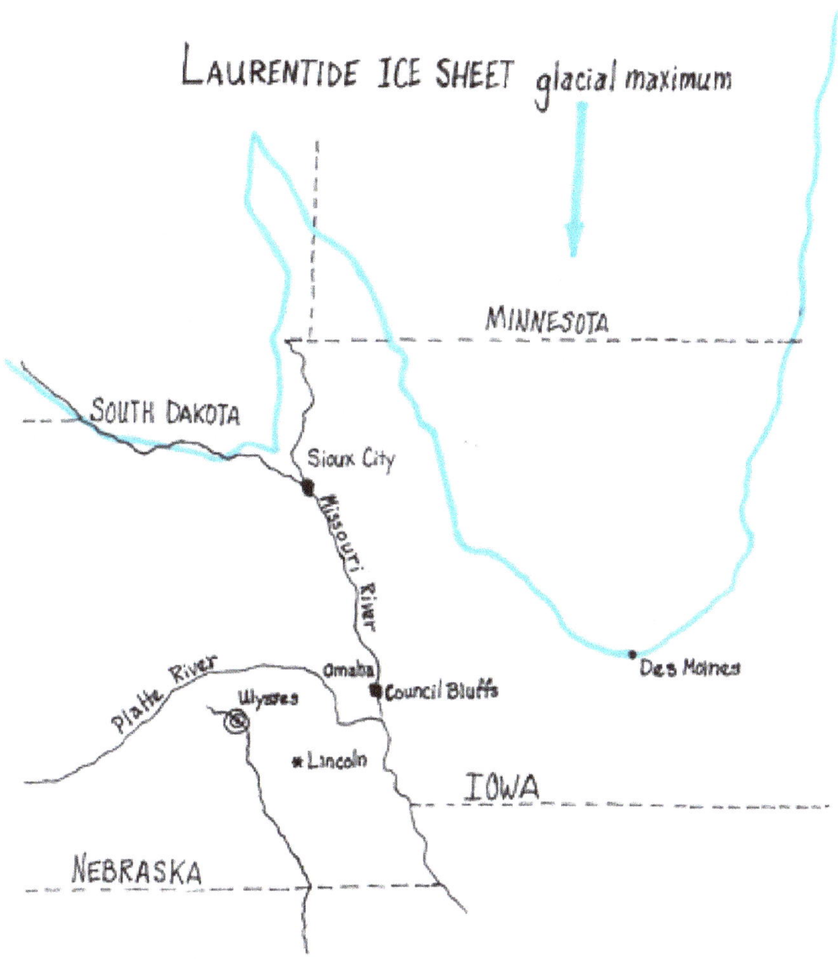

16. Laurentide Ice Sheet glacial maximum